CRITICAL THINKING AND ANALYSIS

PEARSON

We work with leading authors to develop the strongest educational materials in study skills, bringing cutting-edge thinking and best learning practice to a global market.

Under a range of well-known imprints, including Longman, we craft high quality print and electronic publications which help readers to understand and apply their content, whether studying or at work.

To find out more about the complete range of our publishing please visit us on the World Wide Web at: www.pearsoned.co.uk

INSIDE TRACK

CRITICAL THINKING AND ANALYSIS

Mary Deane and Erik Borg

Centre for Academic Writing
Coventry University

Longman
is an imprint of

Harlow, England • London • New York • Boston • San Francisco • Toronto
Sydney • Tokyo • Singapore • Hong Kong • Seoul • Taipei • New Delhi
Cape Town • Madrid • Mexico City • Amsterdam • Munich • Paris • Milan

Pearson Education Limited
Edinburgh Gate
Harlow
Essex CM20 2JE
England

and Associated Companies throughout the world

Visit us on the World Wide Web at:
www.pearsoned.co.uk

First published 2011

ISBN: 978-1-4082-3697-0

British Library Cataloguing-in-Publication Data
A catalogue record for this book is available from the British Library

Library of Congress Cataloging-in-Publication Data
Deane, Mary.
  Critical thinking and analysis / Mary Deane and Erik Borg. -- 1st ed.
      p. cm. -- (Inside track)
  Includes bibliographical references and index.
  ISBN 978-1-4082-3697-0 (pbk.)
 i. Critical thinking. I. Borg, Erik. II. Title.
  BF441.D387 2011
  001.2--dc22
                                              2010030018

10 9 8 7 6 5 4 3 2 1
14 13 12 11 10

Typeset in 9/12.5 pt Helvetica Neue by 3
Printed and bound in Great Britain by Henry Ling Ltd, Dorchester, Dorset

BRIEF CONTENTS

Preface   xi
Introduction   xiii
About the authors   xvi
Acknowledgements   xvii

Part 1 READING   1

1   Everyday critical thinking   3
2   Joining a conversation   13
3   Building on scholarship   27

Part 2 PLANNING   41

4   Components of critical thinking   43
5   A strategy for analysis   53

Part 3 WRITING   63

6   Preparing to write   65
7   Scholarly writing   73

Part 4 REFLECTION   85

8   Reflective critical thinking   87
9   Your career   95
    Conclusion   111
    References   115
    Index   117

CONTENTS

Preface   xi
Introduction   xiii
About the authors   xvi
Acknowledgements   xvii

Part 1 READING   1

1 EVERYDAY CRITICAL THINKING   3

Introduction   4
What is critical thinking?   4
Definitions   4
Key elements in critical thinking   5
Critical thinking in daily life   6
   Asking questions   6
   Asking the right questions   8
   Scepticism   8
Critical thinking in an academic context   8
   The demands of academia   9
Critical thinking is not the same as criticising 10
Critical thinking as your contribution   11
Summary   11
References   12

2 JOINING A CONVERSATION   13

Introduction   14
Reading for references   14
   References in a sample article 14
Examining references   18
   Noticing the names   20
   Noticing the dates   20
Putting the information together   23
Moving forward   23
The SQ3R technique for reading efficiently   25
Summary   26
Reference   26

3 BUILDING ON SCHOLARSHIP   27

Introduction   28
Who me? Building on scholarship   28
   Reading and action   29
Mind the gap   29
   Student writers   30
   Thinking outside the box   30
   Students' knowledge   31
Too descriptive!   32
Examples of critical thinking   33
   Sample assignment 1   33
   Sample assignment 2   34
   Sample assignment 3   35
Where do you stand? Stance in academic writing   36
   Sample assignment 4   37
Summary   39
References   40

Part 2 PLANNING   41

4 COMPONENTS OF CRITICAL THINKING   43

Introduction   44
Components of critical thinking in academia   44
   Connections   45
   Reflectivity   46
   Independence   47
   Time management   48
   Intellectual development   48
   Context   49
   Analysis   49
   Long-term planning   50
Summary   51

5 A STRATEGY FOR ANALYSIS   53

Introduction   54
Generating disciplinary knowledge   54
Using your judgement in academia   55
Descartes' critical thinking method   55
Errors of understanding   56
Errors of academic practice   57
Applications of Descartes' theories   57
   Doubt everything   57

Examine other people's ideas   58

Scepticism is useful   59

Critique your own ideas   59

Analyse texts   60

Revise your writing   60

Talk about your ideas   60

Edit your writing   60

See beyond the surface level   61

Summary   61

References   62

Part 3 WRITING   63

6 PREPARING TO WRITE   65

Introduction   66

Academic assignments   66

Analysing a task   66

Locating and selecting sources   67

Previewing sources   68

Skimming   68

Scanning   68

Writing and disciplinary specificity   69

Conducting research   69

Why read journals to inform your writing?   69

Why persevere?   70

The structure of different journal articles   71

Referencing sources   72

Summary   72

7 SCHOLARLY WRITING   73

Introduction   74

Journal article abstracts   74

Key features of abstracts   75

Key features of articles   76

Analysis of a sample article   77

Introduction   77

Literature review   78

Method   79

Limitations   80

Results   81

Discussion   81

Conclusion   82

To sum up   82

Summary   83
References   83

Part 4 REFLECTION   85

8 REFLECTIVE CRITICAL THINKING   87

Introduction   88
Four steps to help your thinking   88
  1 Look at your questions   89
  2 Do not be closed-minded   89
  3 Clarify your thinking   90
  4 Stick to the point   93
Summary   93
References   93

9 YOUR CAREER   95

Introduction   96
Transferable critical thinking skills   96
  Reflectivity   97
  Independence   97
  Connections   97
Criticality and your career   98
  The job description   98
  Reading the job description critically   100
  Reading the person specification critically   100
  Relating the person specification to yourself   102
Your career ambitions   104
  Skills   104
  Knowledge   104
  Experience   107
Summary   108
References   109

CONCLUSION   111

Reading   111
Planning   112
Writing   112
Reflection   113
Summary   113

References   115
Index   117

PREFACE

This book explores four aspects of critical thinking and analysis:

- Reading
- Planning
- Writing
- Reflection.

These are not the only activities you undertake at university which involve critical thinking and analysis, but as they are core to academic success they are the foci in these chapters. This book is organised into four parts to help you investigate ways of enhancing your performance as you read, plan, write and reflect at university, and in preparation for your chosen profession. Although they are presented as separate, in reality you will engage in all four activities throughout your advanced-level studies. There are many aspects to each of these activities, as illustrated in Figure P1.

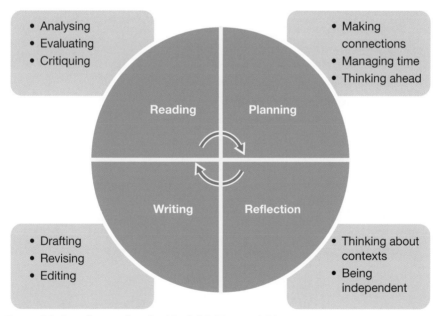

Figure P1 **Four inter-related critical thinking activities**

INTRODUCTION

The aim of this book is to help you develop confidence as a critical thinker, researcher and writer within your academic discipline at university. It is up to you to select from the tips this book contains and adapt them to your own studies because you know best where the practice in your subject area means that you should develop specialist approaches to thinking and writing. Whether you are working in the sciences, humanities or social sciences, there are discipline-specific ways of organising and communicating ideas, which you will learn about as you study, in particular by reading the sources your tutors recommend.

This book is particularly valuable for students making the transition to university who wish to become more familiar with the demands of scholarly research and writing. It also contains useful advice for students moving to a new level of study, especially those undertaking extended projects which require the analysis of texts and the ability to generate and articulate innovative ideas.

ACADEMIC SUCCESS

For the best results as a scholar, try to ensure that constructive criticality underpins every aspect of the way you tackle your projects. You can cultivate your ability to read, write and think analytically by considering the suggestions in this book, but you should also reflect upon ways of making these relevant to the discipline-specific knowledge and skills your tutors expect you to develop. Critical thinking is a vital component of advanced level study which is closely related to:

- **your engagement with other people's ideas**
- **your own creativity as a scholar.**

Research has shown that with commitment and practice, you can enhance your performance and creativity through personal organisation and effective time management (Zampetakis *et al*. 2010: 23). This book addresses some of the main issues you need to consider to enhance your confidence in critical thinking, but the better you know how you operate, the more effective and efficient you will become in producing academic work (Wallas 1926: 5).

In addition to improving your performance by pursuing analytic thinking, you should be aware of your unconscious habits and assumptions. The 'less conscious factors in thought' have a strong impact on your academic performance by influencing how you respond to sources and how you produce your academic writing (Wallas 1926: 5).

This book is divided into four parts:

- **Part 1 Reading**
- **Part 2 Planning**
- **Part 3 Writing**
- **Part 4 Reflection.**

Part One introduces the importance of selecting the best sources for your task and analysing the data they contain. It argues that time is essential to incubate the ideas you absorb and interrogate their reliability for your own academic projects. Remembering your purpose when you are reading and engaging intellectually with the authors will help you to focus your analysis and, with practice, you will develop a mental framework for critiquing the information you encounter as a researcher and writer at university.

Part Two offers ways of conceptualising your critical thinking as a process, whilst stressing that these are not the only ways to approach your studies (Cottrell 2005). As you read this section you can think about the specific requirements of your own academic discipline and determine the best way of organising your time to maximise your efficiency as a scholar in this subject area.

Part Three relates the process of critical thinking to the activity of writing in an analytic style, which is an essential capability at university because you are often assessed by your ability to communicate ideas in writing. As reading academic texts enhances your ability to write in a scholarly manner, this section emphasises how you can learn from examples of good practice in journal articles whilst keeping a critical eye on how the authors articulate their ideas.

Part Four explores how to think reflectively to maximise your effectiveness as a scholar and a professional. It investigates how to analyse a problem and offers some tips on planning for success in your career. Like the rest of the book, this section is just a starting point for your own reflection and you should think about how to adapt and develop the tips for your own activities and goals.

Although *Critical Thinking and Analysis* is divided into four parts, the main message is that reading, planning, writing and reflection are inter-connected in your academic and professional practice, as illustrated in Figure I.1 opposite.

Figure I.1 **Four components of academic and professional success**

As you are reading each section of this book, try to think about the bigger picture and the various ways in which your own reading, planning, writing and reflection at university are opportunities to develop confidence and effectiveness as a scholar.

References

Wallas, G. (1926) *The Art of Thought*. New York: Harcourt Brace.

Zampetakis, L. A., Bouranta, N. and Moustakis, V. S. (2010) On the Relationship between Individual Creativitiy and Time Management. *Thinking Skills and Creativity* 5: 23–32.

ABOUT THE AUTHORS

Dr Mary Deane is a Senior Lecturer in Academic Writing at Coventry University's Centre for Academic Writing. She specialises in discipline-specific writing development, academic practice, publication strategies, rhetorical theory and technologies for learning and teaching. She has published widely on writing pedagogies and staff development.

Dr Erik Borg is a Senior Lecturer in Academic Writing at Coventry University's Centre for Academic Writing. He specialises in academic writing and linguistics. Erik has taught academic writing to students at undergraduate and postgraduate levels in the UK, China and Oman for more than 10 years. He has developed and taught courses on teaching and researching academic writing for Master's students, and has published extensively on academic writing.

ACKNOWLEDGEMENTS

Author's acknowledgements

We would like to thank Steve Temblett, Katy Robinson, and Anita Atkinson of Pearson Education for their expertise. We would also like to thank Linda Dhondy for her work on this book.

We are especially grateful to Michaela Borg for all her expertise. We extend warm thanks to Moira and Pat Deane, Teresa and Tim Fediw, Charley and Tom Gaston, Joe and Paul Deane, Paul Grove, Mollie Joynson-Hewell, Emma Joynson, Josie Facchetti, Sally Jackson, Gwen Dagorne, Yma Choudry, Steve Foster, Neil Gopee, Simon Bell and Sarah Haas.

We are grateful to our colleagues at the Centre for Academic Writing for their great support, in particular Catalina Neculai, Clare Panter, Cynthia Barnes, Dimitar Angelov, Holly Vass, Janet Collinge, Jon Morley, Lisa Ganobcsik-Williams, Magda Ciepalowicz, Miriam Evans, Monica Sharma, Penny Gilchrist, Phil Russell, Ray Summers, Sarah Wilkerson, Sheila Medlock and Tom Parkinson.

Publisher's acknowledgements

We are grateful to the following for permission to reproduce copyright material:

Text

Quote on page 9 from When it comes round to marking assignments: How to impress and how to 'distress' lecturers, *Assessment and Evaluation in Higher Education*, 35, 173–89 (Greasley, P. and Cassidy, A. 2010); Box on page 9 from When it comes round to marking assignments: How to impress and how to distress lecturers, *Assessment and Evaluation in Higher Education*, 35, 182 (Greasley, P. and Cassidy, A. 2010); Box on pages 15–17 from A model of (of ten mixed) stereo-type content: Competence and warmth respectively follow from perceived status and competition, *Journal of Personality and Social Psychology*, 82 878–902 (Fiske, S.T., Cuddy, A.J.C., Glick, P. and Xu, J. 2002); Box on page 19 from A model of (often mixed) stereotype content: Competence and warmth respectively follow from perceived status and competition, *Journal of Personality and Social Psychology*, 82, 879 (Fiske, S.T., Cuddy, A.J.C., Glick, P. and Xu, J. 2002); Box on page 20 from A model of (often mixed) stereotype content: Competence and warmth respectively follow from perceived status and competition, *Journal of Personality and Social Psychology*, 82, 878 (Fiske, S.T., Cuddy, A.J.C., Glick, P. and Xu, J. 2002); Box on page 23 from A model of (often mixed) stereotype content: Competence and warmth respectively follow from perceived status and competition,

Journal of Personality and Social Psychology, 82, 878 (Fiske, S.T., Cuddy, A.J.C., Glick, P. and Xu, J. 2002); Box on page 31 from British Undergraduates make three times as many errors in English as do ones from overseas. Lamb, B. 2009, http://www. clearest.co.uk/files/OverseasUndergraduatesHaveBetterEnglishThanHomeOnes. pdf; Box on page 32 from When it comes round to marking assignments: How to impress and how to 'distress' lecturers, *Assessment and Evaluation in Higher Education*, 35, 180 (Greasley, P. and Cassidy, A. 2010); Sample assignment 2 on pages 34–5 from Gemma Chaplin; Box on page 37 from When it comes round to marking assignments: How to impress and how to 'distress' lecturers, *Assessment and Evaluation in Higher Education*, 35, 182 (Greasley, P. and Cassidy, A. 2010); Sample assignment 4 on page 38 from Sarah Mills; Boxes on page 75, page 76, page 77 from How does information technology shape thinking?, *Thinking Skills and Creativity*, 1, 130 (Barzilai, S. and Zohar, A. 2006); Extract on page 78 from How does information technology shape thinking?, *Thinking Skills and Creativity*, 1, 132 (Barzilai, S. and Zohar, A. 2006); Box on page 79 from How does information technology shape thinking, *Thinking Skills and Creativity*, 1, 133 (Barzilai, S. and Zohar, A. 2006); Box on page 80 from How does information technology shape thinking?, *Thinking Skills and Creativity*, 1, 135, 142 (Barzilai, S. and Zohar, A. 2006); Box on page 82 from How does information technology shape thinking?, *Thinking Skills and Creativity*, 1, 141 (Barzilai, S. and Zohar, A. 2006); Extract on page 82 from How does information technology shape thinking?, *Thinking Skills and Creativity*, 1, 141 (Barzilai, S. and Zohar, A. 2006); Box on page 82 from How does information technology shape thinking? *Thinking Skills and Creativity*, 1, 143 (Barzilai, S. and Zohar, A. 2006); Extract on page 83 from How does information technology shape thinking?, *Thinking Skills and Creativity*, 1, 143 (Barzilai, S. and Zohar, A. 2006); Data collection method box and results box on pages 79–80 from How Does Information Technology Shape Thinking?, *Thinking Skills and Creativity* 1, 130–145 (Barzilai, S. and Zohar, A. 2006).

Figures and tables

Figures 9.2 and 9.3 and Table 9.4 with permission from Leeds City Council.

In some instances we have been unable to trace the owners of copyright material, and we would appreciate any information that would enable us to do so.

PART 1

READING

Researching your topic thoroughly is a vital part of effective critical thinking, that requires you to engage with sources and develop your own perspectives. Before you begin reading, think about your requirements by re-reading any instructions you have been given.

- Check that you understand your task
- Start with the sources your tutors recommend
- Undertake additional independent research
- Get advice from specialists in the university library
- Do not take sources at face value, but analyse the contents
- Make notes of the author, date, page numbers and publication details in order to cite and reference your sources fully.

1 ▶ EVERYDAY CRITICAL THINKING

This chapter explores definitions of critical thinking and invites you to consider your use of criticality both in daily life and in academia. It points out that critical thinking should be a balance of positive and negative points, and that it is not the same as criticising. Crucially, the chapter argues that critical thinking is about making your own contribution as a scholar.

This chapter covers:

- What is critical thinking?
- Definitions
- Key elements in critical thinking
- Critical thinking in daily life
- Critical thinking in an academic context
- Critical thinking is not the same as criticising
- Critical thinking as your contribution.

Using this chapter

Topic	Page
What is critical thinking?	4
Definitions	4
Key elements in critical thinking	5
Critical thinking in daily life	6
Asking questions	6
Asking the right questions	8
Scepticism	8
Critical thinking in an academic context	8
The demands of academia	9
Critical thinking is not the same as criticising	10
Critical thinking as your contribution	11

INTRODUCTION

This chapter investigates what critical thinking is. It explains that, rather than a rare skill only found and used at university, critical thinking is a habit of mind and a skill that you probably use every day. However, this skill needs to be cultivated and applied to all the work that you do at university. This chapter looks at how you practise critical thinking on a day-to-day basis and how you might extend this practice to your work at university.

WHAT IS CRITICAL THINKING?

Take a moment, before reading further in this book, to think about and write down what you believe critical thinking is. We suggest you do this because – and this isn't to give the answer away – taking charge of your thinking is one of the most important elements of critical thinking. Writing down your ideas about critical thinking is a way for you identify what you hope to learn from this book, and that is a long step toward improving your critical thinking. So write down on a piece of paper what you believe critical thinking is. Here are some questions which might help you create your own definition:

■ What led you to pick up this book?
■ When do you use critical thinking?
■ When have you failed to use critical thinking?
■ Is there anything that you need for critical thinking?

As will be suggested later, critical thinking is not the invention of any particular person. All of us use critical thinking, though perhaps without an awareness of being critical and also, perhaps, without being careful to use it regularly. However, the development of thinking about critical thinking is associated with certain figures in history. The Greek philosopher, Socrates (470–399 BCE), questioned the beliefs of his students and fellow citizens to such an extent that his style of thought-provoking investigation became known as 'the Socratic method', and led to him being executed by his fellow Athenians for doubting their religious beliefs. His questioning was a practical form of critical thinking. Acquiring the habit of critical thinking can be life changing, though we hope it will not change your life as it did Socrates'!

DEFINITIONS

However, it was John Dewey (1859–1952), an American philosopher, who is described as the originator of modern thinking about critical thinking. He was a *pragmatist*, a philosopher whose writings focused on the practical nature, effects and outcomes of thought and belief. He distinguished what he called *reflective thinking* from the thoughts that we all have constantly, at least while we are awake. Observations, ideas and recollections go on in our heads, but do not constitute reflective consideration. Reflective thinking 'is marked by acceptance or rejection of something as reasonably probable or improbable' (Dewey 1997/1910: 4), that is, by an effort to make a decision.

Dewey defined reflective thinking as 'active, persistent, and careful consideration of a belief or supposed form of knowledge in the light of the grounds which support it and further conclusions to which it tends' (1997/1910: 6). Dewey's definition highlights the work involved in critical thinking: it must be both active and persistent. This definition also implies that beliefs or knowledge, that is, the ideas that we are considering, must be inspected at their foundations, the underlying ideas that comprise the idea. This type of inspection rules out considering who else holds these beliefs or why, other than their truth, those people might think that way. Finally, Dewey's definition insists that we look at the implications of the belief or form of knowledge, the 'so what?' factor. If, after careful investigation, the knowledge is proved factual, or the belief true, what should be done? Reflective or critical thinking should affect what we do and not just what we think.

Critical thinking

■ Is active and persistent

■ Looks at the reasons for belief

■ Considers the implications of belief that is found to be true.

Later definitions (e.g., Paul and Elder 2002) also suggest that critical thinking is reflective; it thinks about and tries to improve the process of thinking.

Look back now at the definition that you wrote down earlier. How many of these elements did you include in your definition? If you had most of them – perhaps in different forms – congratulations! If you missed important elements, then we hope that this book will help develop your critical thinking skills and show why this capacity is so valuable.

KEY ELEMENTS IN CRITICAL THINKING

In this characterisation of critical thinking, there are elements which need to be highlighted. First, critical thinking is persistent. It should become a habit that you exercise every day. Like many skills, practice will help you get better. Secondly, critical thinking involves asking 'Why?' questions. It looks for evidence, reasons and motivation. Thirdly, critical thinking is active thinking. It is an active process – it's not simply the ideas that float through your head, it involves actively choosing to look at possibilities. Then, when you have come to a decision, you need to act on that

5

decision. Finally, critical thinking involves inspecting your own thinking processes and trying to refine and improve these. You need to consider your own reasons and motivations, and decide whether you acted based on evidence or followed your inclination.

One important point to note about these characteristics is that they are not tied to a particular setting. Critical thinking is not solely an academic skill, though it is certainly valued in academia. Dewey and others who have discussed critical thinking emphasise its day-to-day value, the ways in which critical thinking makes us better able to control our own lives, and help our friends and family and participate as thoughtful citizens. It is also highly prized by employers, who look for employees who do not simply do what is required, but go on to question how they can do better.

CRITICAL THINKING IN DAILY LIFE

Critical thinking is an everyday skill. Most of us practise it day in and day out, without ever labelling what we do 'critical thinking'. Read the e-mail message opposite – you have probably received messages like this from time to time – and think about how you would respond to it.

When you have read the e-mail, ask yourself whether you would contact Mr Peter Makovski, or does the message raise more questions than it answers? Here are some questions which might have occurred to you as you read this message:

- **What is a Transactions Specialist position?**
- **What is minimal experience and knowledge of basic bank operations?**
- **What is good administrative reporting?**
- **Why are they offering so much money for a job that does not require any special qualification?**
- **Why are there three different names (Daine Mech, mr.alex.kovalski and Peter Makovski) connected with this offer?**
- **What does PHC Consulting do? Where is it located?**
- **Why can't the writer compose an e-mail message in accurate English?**

If you asked some of these questions – or others which may have occurred to you – you practised critical thinking.

Asking questions

Most people who have e-mail accounts have become used to receiving messages from people they do not know. These messages offer things which other people or you might want, but you know from other people or from your own experience that they will not be delivered as promised. Most of us develop scepticism about e-mails

Date: Tue, 4 Nov 2010 10:36 PM
From: DaineMech291@mark223.com
To: ebarns@muchmail.com
Subject: **High paid part-time job offer**

PHC Consulting has an opening for a TRANSACTIONS SPECIALIST position.

We do our best to fit all our customers' needs as soon as possible. That's why all are staff is a professionally trained and can solve any problem that occurs on their way.

We are not just a set of people, we are a family. We offer you, our potential colleague, to join us. See below, what we offer you.

General requirements:

• Be at least 21 years old.
• Not special Qualifications Needed.
• Have a minimal experience and knowledge of basic bank operations.
• Ability to maintain confidentially of all information.
• Willingness to work from home, take responsibility, set up and achieve goals.
• The ability to crate good administrative reporting.
• Honesty, responsibility and promptness in operations.
• The ability to operate with more than one task effectively, and have an adaptable, flexible, professional attitude.
• The ability of stable communication with our company and on-time and detailed reporting.
• Familiar to working online, Internet and e-mail skills.

What we offer:

• Generous salary (over 3,000.00 GBP monthly).
• Social benefits and medical insurance.
• Free training and seminars.
• Paid Holidays plus 2 weeks of Paid Time Off (PTO).

This is easy job, but your help is very important for us and our clients. This job does not require any special education. You wouldn't have to pay us for taking you on our list. However we guarantee stable income.

Please send your answer letter or resume to mr.alex.kovalski.phc@cmzp.com

(!) Add our e-mail in your Address Book!!!

Best regards,

Peter Makovski.

http://consultphc.fm.cw

from people we do not know. That is, if we bother to open the messages, we always ask questions about them. That is one key part of critical thinking.

Asking the right questions

The other part is that you knew the right questions to ask because you knew about the world. What you knew might not have been obvious, but it informed your questions. For example, if you asked, 'What is a Transaction Specialist?' you knew that people are seldom offered jobs that they do not understand the name of. If you asked, 'Why are they offering so much money for a job that does not need advanced qualifications?' you knew that most jobs that pay well need training or education. If anyone could do them, anyone would, and they would not pay very much. And if you asked, 'Why are there so many different names of people, but no name for the business?' it was because you knew that businesses offering jobs always identify themselves, but usually give the name of an office or institutional role (e.g., Human Resources, Director of Employment) that applicants should contact.

Scepticism

If you asked questions about the message, you demonstrated scepticism, that is, you raised questions about the senders of the message and their motives. The questions that you asked were related to your knowledge of the world, and developed through your experience of the Internet and e-mail systems, including spam mail.

This knowledge is grounded in your awareness of the way the world works. Few jobs – and fewer well-paid jobs – are offered without carefully targeted advertising. You linked smaller questions that were reasonable to ask, such as 'What is this job?' and 'Who is offering this job?' to a larger question. That question was something like 'Why is a person or company offering a job at a good salary without clearly saying what the company does or what the job is?' That question, in turn, suggests another: 'What might be the motive for someone to offer a job in this way?' Those questions lead to the most likely answer: the job is not real and the people offering the job want something, probably money, from the person who receives the e-mail.

CRITICAL THINKING IN AN ACADEMIC CONTEXT

Critical thinking in an academic context is similar to everyday questioning. It has the same two components:

- a habit of questioning
- specific knowledge.

Most of us ask questions about the events in the world around us. We ask questions like, 'Who told you?' or 'How do you know that?' We question politicians' claims, news sources' assertions and the statements of friends and family, particularly when we disagree with them. However, we tend to turn off our questioning in academic contexts because we too often accept what teachers, textbooks or journal articles tell us. We may do this because of their authority, or because we have learned that passing tests or writing assignments is easier if we repeat to the teacher what they have told us. However, as you move into advanced-level study, expectations change and academics expect you to add value to what is already known – by making your contribution to knowledge.

The demands of academia

Critical thinking in academic contexts requires knowledge developed through study, rather than the knowledge that you have developed through your everyday life using tools like the Internet and e-mail, your awareness of the way jobs are advertised and offered, and your general knowledge. Academics value critical thinking. In a study of issues that impressed and annoyed academics when they marked student assignments, Greasley and Cassidy found that 'too much description, too little critical analysis' was the third most negative item (after 'failing to answer the question' and 'poor language') (2010: 185). The presence of 'critical analysis, perspective, and argument (with supporting evidence)' made the strongest and most favourable impression in students' assignments.

In their discussion of favourable elements, Greasley and Cassidy (2010) quote academics, saying that they looked for the following:

Favourable elements

- Analysis of reading rather than description
- Critical debate supported with appropriate literature
- Critical comment on the literature ('author A takes this view in contrast to author B – what they both fail to account for fully is' ... or – 'an alternative interpretation can be offered by' ... or 'this does not account for the problematic nature of (this concept)', etc.)
- Engaging with the topic at a deeper level and clearly demonstrating an ability to see perspectives and to be able to present these within their assignment and develop reasoned conclusions.

(Greasley and Cassidy 2010: 182)

These responses suggest some of the many ways in which critical thinking plays a part in successful academic assignments. First, critical thinking is a crucial element in students' engagement with sources (e.g., 'analysis of reading rather than description'). Next, when students write, their assignments are seen as stronger when they compare and contrast different sources. This requires both wide-ranging reading and writing that makes the differences between sources clear (e.g., 'author A takes this view in contrast to author B'). Finally, the whole assignment needs to be thought through and informed by critical analysis (e.g., 'engaging with the topic at a deeper level').

CRITICAL THINKING IS NOT THE SAME AS CRITICISING

People who are new to critical thinking sometimes believe that what they need to do is figure out what is wrong with everything, and criticise it. We call this the 'slash and burn' approach to critical thinking – the more problems you can find, the better you are at critical thinking.

However, critical thinking is much more than criticising. Many people (e.g., Bailin and Siegel 2003) feel that critical thinking must have a creative dimension. You need to recognise the inadequacies and problems with other people's ideas, but you also need the ability to find new solutions. Even analysing what other people have said may require 'thinking outside the box'. Frequently, it is necessary to accept that a solution is adequate or practical, even if it is not ideal.

A better approach to critical thinking might be to think of a situation in which you wanted to buy something that was near the limit of your spending ability, such as a computer, a car or agreeing a new mobile contract. You might have considered buying a used computer, car or new mobile. Reflect on the process of consideration that you went through in buying something like this. You knew that what you could get would not be 'perfect'. It would have some problems and some limitations, so you had to go through a process of identifying and prioritising what you wanted to do with the computer, car or phone. What was most important, and what did you want, but could live without?

A purely negative approach would not have been useful. You knew that you could not afford the ideal, and so simply tearing down what you were considering would not help. You needed to consider what the computer, car or phone offered, and what it lacked. You had to understand as well as you could the device you wanted, but you also had to inspect your own thinking. What did you need, and what could be dropped or accepted as alright?

This is critical thinking. Simply criticising would not have been adequate; you needed to reflect on your own thinking and your own desires. It was an active process, and it was directed toward making a decision – you were going to buy something that might not be perfect, because it did what you needed to do, or, possibly, you were going to walk away and wait till you could afford exactly what you needed. Making the decision involved both knowledge and analysis, and possibly looking for another solution. In any case, your critical thinking was very different from criticising.

CRITICAL THINKING AS YOUR CONTRIBUTION

Critical thinking means much more than reading and criticising the work of other people. It means **adding value** to your learning process and the knowledge that other people have. Critical thinking is a process of identifying what is not known and actively looking for information that will answer those questions. As in other cases that we have discussed, critical thinking is an everyday skill. It should be exercised in your studies, of course, but it should be something you do all the time.

One of us (Erik) was a photographer before becoming an academic. He had a contract to photograph artworks for a book, but the artworks were privately owned and had to be photographed in the owners' homes, and the homes were scattered over 50 miles, north and south. Erik would contact the owners and set up appointments to come and photograph their artworks. The photography could take a few hours, as lights and background had to be set up, but the travel time had to be accounted for as well. With the long distances that needed to be travelled, it was important to group works that were near to each other.

Erik's assistant, a university undergraduate working part-time for him, realised that they were often late in getting to the art owners. She recognised that Erik was regularly too optimistic about how long it would take to photograph an object and about how long it would take to pack up and get to the home of the next owner. She recognised the problem and brought this to Erik's attention, offering to make the appointments for them. Her thinking was more effective than his in this case. She recognised the problem and its cause, and offered a solution. They got to the appointments that she made on time.

In a similar way, you should be critically analysing the situations around you and considering their underlying causes. Then you should consider how you could make changes that will improve the situation. That is successful critical thinking.

SUMMARY

This chapter has suggested that critical thinking is not a special academic skill, but a day-to-day activity that we all need and use in many contexts. However, it is important to bring the critical thinking skills that we have to academic contexts, and to sharpen them for academic work. Critical thinking, as practised in daily life and in the university, is not the same as constantly criticising; instead, it is a way for you to add value and make a contribution.

The main arguments in this chapter were:

- Critical thinking is active and persistent; it looks for reasons, considers implications and is reflective
- Critical thinking is an everyday skill, as well as an academic practice
- Critical thinking is a way for you to contribute to knowledge in your field.

References

Bailin, S. and Siegel, H. (2003) Critical Thinking. In Blake, N., Smeyers, P., Smith, R. and Standish, P. (eds) *The Blackwell Guide to the Philosophy of Education.* Oxford: Blackwell: 181–193.

Dewey, J. (1997/1910) *How We Think*. Mineola, NY: Dover Publications.

Greasley, P. and Cassidy, A. (2010) When it Comes Round to Marking Assignments: How to Impress and How to 'Distress' Lecturers. *Assessment and Evaluation in Higher Education* 35: 173–189.

Paul, R. and Elder, L. (2002) *Critical Thinking: Tools for Taking Charge of your Personal and Professional Life*. Upper Saddle River, NJ: Financial Times Prentice Hall.

2 ▶ JOINING A CONVERSATION

This chapter further examines how to make a contribution as a scholar by joining in the conversation within your chosen subject area. It examines how to read for references by noticing authors' names and publication dates so you can put information together in an analytic way. The chapter offers tips on reading efficiently and developing a clear purpose as you explore the literature in your field.

This chapter covers:

- Reading for references
- Examining references
- Putting the information together
- Moving forward
- The SQ3R technique for reading efficiently.

Using this chapter

Topic	Page
Reading for references	14
References in a sample article	14
Examining references	18
Noticing the names	20
Noticing the dates	21
Putting the information together	23
Moving forward	23
The SQ3R technique for reading efficiently	25

INTRODUCTION

Academic writing is a process of entering an on-going conversation. In everyday life, when you join friends who are having a discussion, you listen for a while to learn what they are talking about, and then you try to add something that you know about the topic that they are discussing. In a similar way in academic life, you need to learn about the topic under discussion before you can comment. Your contribution to the conversation, though, is ultimately what is important for you and the subject that you are studying.

This chapter discusses how you can join in the conversation of your discipline, and learn to contribute to the discussion. The discussions that are carried out in academic texts are designed to help you participate, but you need to learn how to use the information that you are given. To participate, you need to understand the background and the issues which are being discussed. That understanding will be gained by reading in your discipline, and particularly by reading beyond the texts which are suggested or assigned for your courses. It is up to you to find relevant and appropriate readings and bring them to the conversation.

READING FOR REFERENCES

In order to understand how professional writers use sources to create the context for their writing, you must read enough of a text to understand the story that the writers are trying to tell. The extract reproduced in the Quiz below will be used throughout this chapter to illustrate how you can enter an on-going conversation by understanding the references that the writers provide.

The extract is from a journal article 'A Model of (often mixed) Stereotype Content: Competence and Warmth Respectively Follow from Perceived Status and Competition' by Fiske, Cuddy, Glick and Xu, which was published in *The Journal of Personality and Social Psychology* in 2002. This article discusses how we form stereotypes of groups of people who are different from us. Read the extract below from this article first to understand what is being said, then answer the extract questions at the end to help you check that you have understood the, then answer the extract. The paragraphs have been numbered to aid the discussion of this extract.

References in a sample article

QUIZ

Read the extract from Fiske, Cuddy, Glick and Xu (2002) opposite.

1 Not all stereotypes are alike. Some stereotyped groups are disrespected as incapable and useless (e.g., elderly people), whereas others are respected for excessive, threatening competence (e.g., Asians). Some stereotyped groups are liked as sweet and harmless (e.g., housewives), whereas others are disliked as cold and inhuman (e.g., rich people). Surely, such differences matter.

2 However, social psychology of late has eschewed the study of stereotype content, focusing instead on stereotyping processes (for reviews, see Brown 1995, Fiske 1998, Leyens, Yzerbyt and Schadron 1994, Macrae and Bodenhausen 2000). And for good reason. Stereotyping processes respond to systematic principles that generalize across different specific instances of stereotypes, so the processes invite social–psychological investigation, because they are presumably stable over time, place, and out-group. If the contents of stereotypes come and go with the winds of social pressures, then no single stereotype remains stable and predictable from theoretical principles.

3 Alternatively, if stereotypes do come and go with the winds of social pressures, maybe we can understand those wind patterns and, thus, some origins of stereotype content. In short, perhaps we need a model that predicts the intergroup weather: stereotype content may respond to systematic principles, just as stereotyping processes do.

4 If stereotype content responds to principles, then the first principle must identify common dimensions of content. Following Allport (1954), social psychologists have typically viewed only unflattering stereotypes as indicating prejudice, where prejudice is a uniform antipathy or contempt toward an out-group across a variety of dimensions. Flattering stereotypes have presumably targeted in-groups or, when they target out-groups, have presumably indicated compunction stemming from modern egalitarian ideals.

5 We argue instead that stereotypes are captured by two dimensions (warmth and competence) and that subjectively positive stereotypes on one dimension do not contradict prejudice but often are functionally consistent with unflattering stereotypes on the other dimension. Moreover, we argue that two variables long identified as important in intergroup relations – status and competition – predict dimensions of stereotypes. We suggest that for subordinate, noncompetitive groups (e.g., elderly people), the positive stereotype of warmth acts jointly with the negative stereotype of low competence to maintain the advantage of more privileged groups. For high-status, competitive out-groups (e.g., Asians), the positive stereotype of their competence justifies the overall system but acts jointly with the negative stereotype of low warmth to justify the in-group's resentment of them.

6 Finally, we argue that different combinations of stereotypic warmth and competence result in unique intergroup emotions – prejudices – directed toward various kinds of groups in society. Pity targets the warm but not competent subordinates; envy targets the competent but not warm competitors; contempt is reserved for out-groups deemed neither warm nor competent.

7 Each of these issues – focus on dimensions of content, mixed (but functionally consistent) content, predictions of that content, and ensuing types of prejudice – follows precedents set by previous literature. Our innovation is to synthesize these insights into a model of stereotype content that cuts across out-groups.

Focus on Content: Competence and Warmth

8 Unencumbered by theory, the classic study of stereotype contents (D. Katz and Braly 1933) was replicated at Princeton over about 20-year intervals (G. M. Gilbert 1951, Karlins, Coffman and Walters 1969, Leslie, Constantine and Fiske 2001). These studies document changes in the favorability (mostly improving) and uniformity (decreasing) of stereotypes over time but do not uncover dimensions or principles therein. Although the Katz–Braly checklist method has limitations (Devine and Elliot 1995; Madon *et al.* 2001), it does provide one of the few consistently documented measures of stereotypes across groups.[1] However, the Katz–Braly lineage does not claim theoretical roots.

9 From a functional, pragmatic perspective (Fiske 1992, 1993b), we suggest that dimensions of stereotypes result from interpersonal and intergroup interactions. When people meet others as individuals or group members, they want to know what the other's goals will be vis à vis the self or in-group and how effectively the other will pursue those goals. That is, perceivers want to know the other's intent (positive or negative) and capability; these characteristics correspond to perceptions of warmth and competence, respectively.

10 A variety of work on intergroup and interpersonal perception suggests the relevance of these two dimensions in social perception. In the intergroup domain, early on, one ethnic out-group (i.e., Jews) was viewed as competent but not warm, and another (i.e., 'Negroes') was viewed as warm but not competent (Allport 1954, Bettelheim and Janowitz 1950). Curiously, this older ethnic-group distinction echoes modern-day views about perceived subgroups of women (Deaux, Winton, Crowley and Lewis 1985, Eckes 1994, Noseworthy and Lott 1984, Six and Eckes 1991): disliked, dominant, competent, nontraditional women (e.g., career women, feminists, lesbians, athletes) versus likable, dependent, incompetent, traditional women (e.g., housewives, sometimes 'chicks'). Overall, the ethnic and gender distinctions both fit our hypothesized dimensions of competence and warmth.

11 From various out-group stereotypes, Fiske and Glick (Fiske 1998: 380, Fiske, Xu, Cuddy and Glick 1999, Glick and Fiske 1999, 2001b) constructed a preliminary model of stereotype content: stereotype content may not reflect simple evaluative antipathy but instead may reflect separate dimensions of (dis)like and (dis)respect. Some out-group stereotypes (e.g., housewives, disabled people, elderly people) elicit disrespect for perceived lack of compe-

---

[1] Case studies of specific groups (e.g., Americans, Sisley 1970, Blacks, Devine and Elliot 1995; see Fiske 1998, for others) document continuity and change over time but do not provide comparable measures across groups.

tence; other out-group stereotypes elicit dislike for perceived lack of warmth (e.g., Asians, Jews, career women). Although some groups may elicit both dislike and disrespect (e.g., welfare recipients), qualitative differences among stereotypes are captured by the crucial dimensions of competence and warmth.

12 The plausibility of competence and warmth as core dimensions also springs from person perception research: Asch's (1946) warm–cold versus competence-related adjectives (Hamilton and Fallot 1974, Zanna and Hamilton 1977) and multidimensional scaling of trait descriptions (Rosenberg, Nelson and Vivekanathan 1968; see also Jamieson, Lydon, and Zanna 1987, Lydon, Jamieson and Zanna 1988). Perceptions of individuals in groups also vary along a task dimension and a social dimension (Bales 1970). Relatedly, Peeters (1983, 1992, 1995) has argued for the dimensions of self-profitability (e.g., confident, ambitious, practical, intelligent) – akin to competence – and other-*profitability* (e.g., conciliatory, tolerant, trustworthy) – akin to warmth. The Peeters distinction has been applied to national stereotypes (Peeters 1993, Phalet and Poppe 1997, Poppe and Linssen 1999)[2], values (Wojciszke 1997), and evaluations of social behavior (Vonk 1999).

13 Across racial prejudice, gender subgroups, national stereotypes, and person perception, thus, come two dimensions. They fit the functional idea that people want to know others' intent (i.e., warmth) and capability to pursue it (i.e., competence). Groups (like individuals) are distinguished according to their potential impact on the in-group (or the self). Our stereotype content model's first hypothesis hence holds that perceived competence and warmth differentiate out-group stereotypes.

(Fiske, Cuddy, Glick and Xu 2002: 878–902)

[2] The Phalet and Poppe (1997) work supported two bipolar dimensions, which they termed competence and morality, but morality included honest, helpful, and tolerant – socially warm traits.

1 What is the major claim in this passage?

2 The article says that there are two ways to study stereotyping. What are these?

3 Which of the two ways to study stereotyping does this article use?

4 In Figure 2.1 on p.18, what would be the qualities of the group in the upper left quadrant?

5 According to the authors, what group of people might be stereotyped as belonging to that quadrant?

6 How do people evaluate members of other groups when they first meet them?

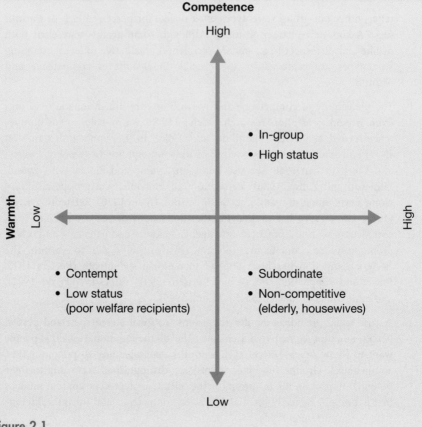

Figure 2.1

EXAMINING REFERENCES

To some extent, reading an academic source such as the Fiske, Cuddy, Glick and Xu article is like those television programmes or mystery novels that are based on forensic scientists figuring out who committed a crime by analysing the evidence that remains at the scene of the crime. The forensic scientists use the clues to build up a picture of the people who might have committed the crime. In the case of an academic text, the evidence is in the references. The references allow the reader to see how the ideas that form the background to the paper were assembled, and allow readers to evaluate those ideas for themselves. Looking at the references that an author has assembled then becomes similar to checking a suspect's alibi. The author quotes or summarises an earlier writer, and as a reader you can ask whether that earlier writer actually wrote what the author claims. You can also check whether the earlier writer had other ideas about the topic which you can use, or simply more information that you can connect to form your own picture of the topic you are investigating.

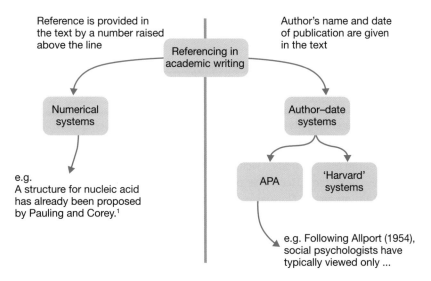

Reference is provided in the text by a number raised above the line

Referencing in academic writing

Author's name and date of publication are given in the text

Numerical systems

Author–date systems

e.g.
A structure for nucleic acid has already been proposed by Pauling and Corey.[1]

APA

'Harvard' systems

e.g. Following Allport (1954), social psychologists have typically viewed only ...

Figure 2.2 **The referencing system**

The referencing system (Figure 2.2) connects the reader to the sources that form the background to an academic text. One of two referencing systems is generally used as Figure 2.2 demonstrates, these are numerical systems and author-date systems. Some disciplines, in particular science-related disciplines, use numeric referencing styles in which sources are cited in the text with numbers raised above the line (e.g. 'as shown[1]') and the sources listed at the end of the article in the order in which they are mentioned in the text.

Other disciplines, such as the social sciences, use an author-date referencing style. In the author–date referencing style, such as the one used in the article, the authors' names and the year of publication of the source are provided in brackets in the text.

An example of the author-date system occurs in paragraph 8 of the journal article:

Unencumbered by theory, the classic study of stereotype contents (D. Katz and Braly 1933) was replicated at Princeton over about 20-year intervals (G. M. Gilbert 1951, Karlins, Coffman, and Walters 1969, Leslie, Constantine, and Fiske 2001).

(Fiske, Cuddy, Glick and Xu 2002: 879)

The authors' names are given in the text, along with the date of their article. The full information needed to find the source is listed in an alphabetic list at the end of the article or book. Katz's initial is given to distinguish him from another Katz who is also cited in Fiske, Cuddy, Glick and Xu (2002).

Sometimes the authors' names are used in the sentence, in which case only the date is put in brackets as in paragraph 4 of the article.

> Following Allport (1954), social psychologists have typically viewed only…
>
> (Fiske, Cuddy, Glick and Xu 2002: 878)

Author–date referencing styles allow the reader to see who is being cited and when they wrote the source that is being cited.

The extract from Fiske, Cuddy, Glick and Xu has 38 separate references (including two that are repeated). Read the extract again, this time noting how some of the names are repeated. Note also the range of dates that you find in the article (remember that the article by Fiske, Cuddy, Glick and Xu was published in 2002).

Noticing the names

Notice the repeated names in the references. These include the authors of the article itself ('A model of (often mixed) stereotype content') (e.g., Fiske 1994, Glick and Fiske 1999) but also include Peeters (e.g., 1983 1992, 1995) and Zanna (e.g., Lydon, Jamison and Zanna 1987, Zanna and Hamilton 1977). Notice that when authors publish together, they frequently change the order of the names, as when Jamieson, Lydon and Zanna published first one paper as Jamieson, Lydon and Zanna (1987) and then followed that with another as Lydon, Jamieson and Zanna (1988). Academic writers often do this when they write more than one article from a single research project. The first author position is most important, as citations are often reduced to (First Author *et al.* 2002). The first author is often called the *lead author*. Sometimes only the lead author's name is given in the text, though the other authors are usually listed in the list of references. In order to be fair to all the researchers working on a project, the names are rotated in different publications.

Notice, too, that one author may publish with more than one other author, as Edwin Poppe did. He published with Phalet (Phalet and Poppe 1997) and with Linssen (Poppe and Linssen 1999). The lead author of this article has published many papers on stereotyping, alone and with other members of the group who wrote this paper (e.g., Fiske 1998, Glick and Fiske 1999, Fiske, Xu, Cuddy and Glick 1999).

Noticing the names of writers who are cited in articles that you read is the first step towards seeing these writers as people who are interested in the topic of stereotyping. These are people who are having an on-going discussion about stereotyping, one that you can join in with. In addition, when you think of them as people rather than disembodied academic journal articles or books, you can begin to accept that they are people who may have a particular way of seeing the world, and that perspective may or may not be one that you share. Since they are people, they can make mistakes, too.

Noticing the dates

As mentioned above, author–date referencing styles also provide the year that the source was published in the text. This serves two purposes: the first is simply to distinguish one source from another source by the same author (e.g., Fiske 1992, Fiske 1998). If an author publishes two papers in a year, a lower case letter is added after the date (e.g., Fiske 1993b).

The second purpose is more important for critical thinking. By providing the date, you can immediately evaluate how old the source is. Many disciplines follow a version of the scientific model of research, in which a source is reviewed and published, and then tested by people in the field. If the theories, practices (such as the methodology) or claims are found to work, the source is accepted, and new work builds on the findings of the publication. This is sometimes called 'a moving front of knowledge' (Figure 2.3). That means that, like explorers travelling up a river toward its source, gradually more of what was unknown territory becomes known. As a result, in many disciplines, newer articles are presumed to build on older articles and, simply put, newer is generally assumed to be better than old. However, in some disciplines, classic ideas and theories are regularly referred to.

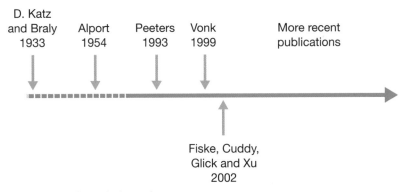

Figure 2.3 **How knowledge advances**

Fiske, Cuddy, Glick and Xu (2002) is somewhat unusual in that it is trying to establish a new synthesis of research and thinking about stereotypes. In order to establish its synthesis, the authors review the literature in great depth. The oldest citation in the passage is D. Katz and Braly (1933). The authors introduce this source in paragraph 8, where they call it 'a classic study', but also say that it was written 'unencumbered by theory'. That latter phrase suggests that it is to some extent naïve and not as well thought through as later papers.

Another older paper that the authors of 'A Model of (often mixed) Stereotype Content' refer to is Allport (1954). This source is introduced in paragraph 4, and mentioned again in paragraph 10. As previously mentioned, in paragraph 4, the authors write:

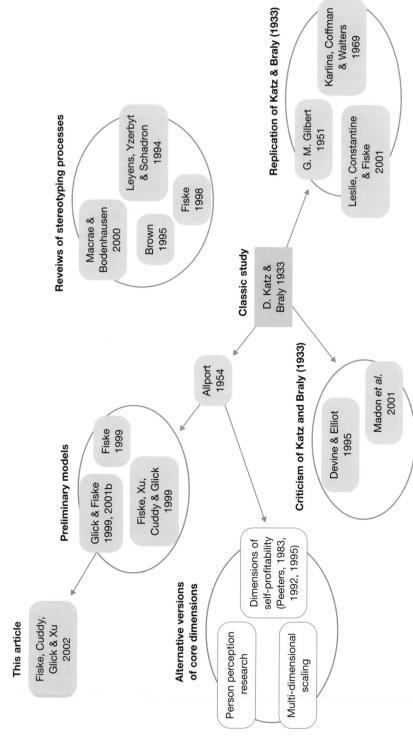

Figure 2.4 A mind map of the literature review of Fiske, Cuddy, Glick and Xu (2002)

> Following Allport (1954), social psychologists have typically viewed only unflattering stereotypes as indicating prejudice...
>
> (Fiske, Cuddy, Glick and Xu 2002: 878)

Note that, on the one hand, the authors suggest that most social psychologists have followed or agreed with Allport (1954). This suggests the classic nature of this paper. On the other hand, the phrase, 'have typically viewed only unflattering stereotypes as indicating prejudice', suggests that there is a gap in which they plan to build their claim. Flattering stereotypes can also indicate prejudice, as when a group is thought to be competent (but not warm) or warm (but not competent).

Of course, most of the references in the Fiske, Cuddy, Glick and Xu (2002) article are not as old as these. Many of the sources, in particular those written by the authors of this article (e.g., Leslie, Constantine and Fiske 2002, Glick and Fiske 2001b), were quite recent when this article was originally published, and indicate that this was a developing area of interest at the time.

You can use the dates to focus your reading. You would probably find that the older publications are covered in more recent texts, so that D. Katz and Braly's (1933) ideas and those of Allport (1954) are covered in textbooks or in review articles such as this article by Fiske, Cuddy, Glick and Xu (2002). On the other hand, articles that are more recent give you alternative perspectives on the topic, and alternative perspectives are at the core of critical thinking.

PUTTING THE INFORMATION TOGETHER

No one expects you to systematically analyse the patterns of citations in a text that you are reading. Instead, you should be aware of these patterns, such as names that are repeated, dates that are unusual, etc. Figure 2.4 (opposite) is a partial mind map of the literature reviewed in Fiske, Cuddy Glick and Xu (2002).

In this map, there is a clear movement from D. Katz and Braly (1933) through Allport (1954) towards the article that is being written. The literature that the authors review is being used to create an argument. To the side of the main path are reviews of studies of stereotyping processes (paragraph 2) and a group of alternative analyses that support the article's claim that prejudice can be mapped on two dimensions, one of warmth and one of competence (paragraph 12).

MOVING FORWARD

In the past, one of the most difficult challenges for scholars was to move forward in the literature. Academics had to follow particular journals in their area carefully in order to know what work was being done. Conferences, too, provided opportunities for academics to learn about new research in their area. However, in almost every area there has been an explosion of information, with more journals and other publications coming out each year. It has become difficult for any scholar to keep up with everything that is being published in her or his area.

If you are new to a discipline you may have more difficulty. You may be given an article, such as Fiske, Cuddy, Glick and Xu (2002), to read, or you may find an article like this and want to know what has been written since the time that the article was published. Publications that cite the article you are reading allow you to enter into the discussion going on about the topic (such as stereotyping, in the case of the article we have used as an example). Hearing a variety of voices on a topic is the first step towards critical thinking.

New tools have become available which facilitate searching for publications that comment on the article you are reading. The most important of these are electronic databases that allow systematic searches of a wide variety of sources. Many of them focus on particular disciplines or wider fields, such as the humanities, social sciences or sciences. The databases that will be available to you will depend to some extent on your university's library service. You should become familiar with them by consulting the subject librarian in your own discipline.

Other sources of information include Google, although that tends to find too many sources, and many of those sources are not reliable. Google Scholar (http://scholar. google.co.uk/) filters its results for academic sources. It also provides information about how frequently a source has been cited, and it has links to those articles. This information can be used to find more recent publications on the same topic, since they would not have cited the article if it was not relevant to their discussion. The article by Fiske, Cuddy, Glick and Xu (2002) has been cited 498 times, according to this search on Google Scholar (Figure 2.5).

Most journals now have Internet pages which link to individual articles, and these pages frequently provide links to publications that have cited the article. In addition, if you find an author who is frequently cited on the topic that you are investigating, you may be able to check their website and find other publications on the same topic. These may be more recent than the publication that you have. All of these

Figure 2.5 **Google Scholar**

provide ways for you to enter the conversation about the topic you are investigating and to begin to contribute to the debates.

THE SQ3R TECHNIQUE FOR READING EFFICIENTLY

You will quickly find that there is more information out there than you can easily deal with. One technique that has been suggested for improving your critical reading skills and your retention of what you have read is called 'Survey, Question, Read, Recall, Review' (SQ3R) (Figure 2.6).

- **S**urvey: determine what the text is about – read table of contents, look at the index
- **Q**uestion: what are the questions you hope the text will answer?
- **R**ead the text carefully, and take bibliographic information for your records
- **R**ecall: what were the most important or most relevant points for your study?
- **R**eview: go back to the text and check that you have remembered the main points correctly.

Using the SQ3R technique will help you check that you have understood what you read. It is a careful and possibly time-consuming process. However, when you are new to an area, when you extend yourself into areas that you are less familiar with, or when you recognise that a source you are reading is important to your area, the SQ3R technique will force you to read carefully. It is not something that you have to do for all your reading, though reflecting and making sure that you understand what you have read is always important.

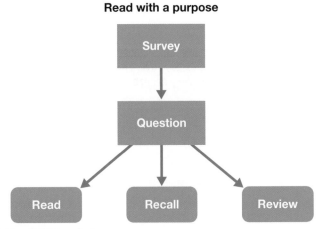

Read with a purpose

Figure 2.6 **The SQ3R technique**

SUMMARY

This chapter has explored how to read for references, recognise names and recognise dates in order to improve your awareness of the literature in your academic field. The main message of this chapter is that you should take every opportunity to join the scholarly conversation in your discipline by thinking critically about the sources you read.

The main arguments in this chapter were:

- Look for clues in the sources you read
- Learn from the ways in which academic authors draw on the literature
- Get to know the main names in your field.

Answers to quiz questions on p.17

1 This article brings together three discrete issues (paragraphs 4, 5 and 6) to create a new understanding of stereotype content that can be used to describe different out-groups (paragraph 7).
2 Stereotyping can be studied as a process, or it can be studied based on the content of the stereotypes (paragraph 2).
3 This article studies the content of stereotypes (paragraph 3).
4 Low warmth, high competence.
5 Rich people (paragraph 1), Asians (paragraph 5), Jews, career women (paragraph 11).
6 Groups are evaluated according to the group's intent toward the in-group (warmth), and how effective they will be in pursuing that intention (competence) (paragraph 9).

Reference

Fiske, S. T., Cuddy, A. J. C., Glick, P. and Xu, J. (2002) A Model of (often mixed) Stereotype Content: Competence and Warmth Respectively follow from Perceived Status and Competition. *Journal of Personality and Social Psychology* 82: 878–902.

3 BUILDING ON SCHOLARSHIP

This chapter continues to examine how you can make a contribution as a scholar by building on existing research. It addresses the difficulty of critiquing sources and offers advice about identifying the limitations of the sources you read in order to help you to develop your own stance as an academic writer.

This chapter covers:

- Who me? Building on scholarship
- Mind the gap
- Too descriptive!
- Examples of critical thinking
- Where do you stand? Stance in academic writing.

Using this chapter

Topic	Page
Who me? Building on scholarship	28
Reading and action	29
Mind the gap	29
Student writers	30
Thinking outside the box	30
Students' knowledge	31
Too descriptive!	32
Examples of critical thinking	33
Sample assignment 1	33
Sample assignment 2	34
Sample assignment 3	35
Where do you stand? Stance in academic writing	36
Sample assignment 4	37

INTRODUCTION

We have tried to emphasise that critical thinking is an active skill. When you read, you need to maintain a questioning stance and ask questions such as:

- What is my purpose in reading this?
- Is it relevant to my needs?
- What is the basis for the claims that are being made here?
- If these claims are true, what does it mean for the decisions I have to make?

Critical thinking as an active skill involves not simply gathering and evaluating information, important as these activities are. Critical thinking is a tool for you to get involved in knowledge creation and make your own contribution to knowledge. In this chapter, we will discuss how you can use your reading to build on existing scholarship.

WHO ME? BUILDING ON SCHOLARSHIP

Students often think that academics do not want to hear their ideas. They may think that academics want them to reproduce – as accurately as possible – what they have learned in their lectures and from their assigned readings. However, that is not usually the case. Although there are areas in which accurately reproducing knowledge is critical and will be tested, often this occurs at the beginning of learning a new area or discipline. As you become more knowledgeable in an area, your tutors want to know *what you can do with your knowledge*, what you can contribute.

Tutors do not want uninformed speculation. At university you should produce ideas with more basis than you could expect by asking the people who happened to be on a cross-town bus. Your ideas must be based on what you have learned through your studies, but then your ideas should increase or refine what is already known. One lecturer in Human Resource Management spoke of this in terms of the two large groups of students he had on his courses. He made this observation:

> Overseas students have a perception that what you want from them is the right answer, and that right answer is to be found in books, and therefore they will give you the books, 'cause that's surely what you want.
>
> UK students tend to almost an opposite point of view, which is what you want from them is their opinion, with zero reference to any books… actually, we have an academic model of what we expect from them, which is somewhere in the middle, and these students, who are UK and overseas, are on opposite sides of it, and we're trying to bring both of them into the middle.
>
> (Lecturer from Human Resources Management 2010)

These comments from the lecturer generalise broadly about overseas and UK students. According to this view, both overseas and UK students exercise critical thinking skills, whilst some overseas students give opinions without basing them on solid information and some UK students give information from their reading without considering it critically. Perhaps it is best to avoid generalisations, while accepting that what tutors want (most of the time) is informed judgement.

Reading and action

At university, many marking schemes reflect tutors' desire for an informed contribution that will build on existing knowledge. For example, the marking criteria listed in Table 3.1 describe the qualities expected at distinction level for undergraduate study.

Reading	Action
Evidence of wide-ranging reading and/or research	Independent, critical thought
Demonstrates wide reading around the subject, both in printed and web-based form	Demonstrates an ability to identify key issues in a debate and critically assess, reflect upon and contextualise the evidence and arguments related to that debate
Shows a rigorous use and a good understanding of relevant source materials	Evidence of initiative and independent thought
Good use of secondary literature	Evidence of developing capacity for independent thought with respect to ideas, aims and approach
Shows clear evidence of wide and relevant reading and an engagement with the conceptual issues	Contains evidence of sound independent thinking, presenting material in an original fashion

Table 3.1 **Sample marking criteria**

These criteria suggest what tutors may be looking for when they read assignments. They want evidence that students have carefully read and absorbed not only the readings that they have suggested, but also that they have gone beyond those readings to find other relevant sources that throw light on the topic. They also want these readings to be brought together in a way that shows independent thinking.

MIND THE GAP

As you study the literature in your field, you should be asking yourself, 'What is my purpose in reading this?' In the relatively recent past, say, 30 years ago, finding information on a topic was difficult and it required extended searches in the library which were limited by the size of the library. Now the challenge is to find the bit of information that you need when so much information is quickly available, especially online. The analogy of drinking from a fire hose is sometimes used to express the overwhelming volume of information that is available on any conceivable topic. In order to keep your focus clear, keep asking, 'Why am I reading this?'

In part, you are reading to gain an understanding of the field, to pick up knowledge that you did not have previously. In part, though, you are reading in order to find out what other people also do not know. This is where your own contribution will grow. After describing what is known, summarising as carefully as possible and highlighting the points that are relevant to your argument, you will need to say what you have found out.

Student writers

Student writers frequently have difficulty at this stage, for two reasons. First, they may lack confidence in critiquing published writers who might be senior academics. Students tell themselves something like, 'They've been studying this topic for years; how can I think I've come up with a problem that they haven't answered already?' Secondly, student writers sometimes worry that they do not have any basis for questioning the information that they read in academic articles. They know that they have not conducted experiments or interviewed participants.

These worries can be addressed by critical thinking skills. Critical thinking is democratic. If you think clearly, it does not matter whether you are a student or an academic, you can question what other people say. And, although you may not have conducted formal experiments, you have your own experience that you can draw upon.

Thinking outside the box

Academics occasionally describe their own experiences of questioning – or failing to question – what they read. Laurie Taylor, a sociologist at Birkbeck College, University of London, described how he started studying psychology at university. When he started, psychology was dominated by behaviourism, the belief that psychological knowledge could only advance by studying people's behaviour, rather than trying to understand what went on in their minds. Behaviourists felt that the best way to understand human behaviour was to study how rats responded to conditioning: that is, by rewarding rats with food (or punishing them) to see how quickly they changed their behaviour in response to the rewards or punishment. See what Taylor (2010) wrote about this on the page opposite.

In this passage, Taylor admits that he failed to compare what he was learning with what he already knew about people when he started studying psychology as an undergraduate. In the whole article, he goes on to explain that he knew that people did not simply act based on rewards and punishment, but also out of curiosity, malice and generosity, among other motivations that could not be reduced to punishment and rewards. Taylor began to revise his opinions of behaviourism when he read a critical book review by the linguist, Noam Chomsky, that made him reconsider what he had been taught.

But within weeks of beginning my studies in 1960, I found myself plunged into a version of psychology that seemed about as relevant to understanding human beings as marine biology. For my arrival at Birkbeck coincided with the rise of behaviourism... It was, I believe, my nervousness about being at university that inclined me to adopt behaviourism and all its tenets with unqualified enthusiasm. *It no more occurred to me to bring what I already knew about the world to bear upon what I was being taught* than it would occur to a novitiate monk to start questioning the truths of Christianity.

(Taylor 2010: 43 emphasis added)

Taylor's experience of re-evaluating his own knowledge and experience after reading an academic source is similar to the experience of many students. Critical thinking depends on subject knowledge – developed through wide reading – and reflection on our own experiences. Both parts, reflection and knowledge, are necessary for critical thinking.

Students' knowledge

Look at the paragraphs below in which a lecturer in genetics at Imperial College London (Lamb 2009) reflects upon his students' knowledge of grammar, spelling and punctuation.

Students' knowledge

On average, home students made three times more errors in English than did the overseas students, who had been taught better, had been corrected much more often, and who took English more seriously than did the home students. The latter's attitude was often, 'Well, you know what I meant.' In some Asian countries, a student's social standing goes up as his or her marks go up, but success is often looked down on here. One of the students from Singapore told me that they regarded any mark of less than 70% as a failure, and that they had been reared in a very competitive environment. UK students often boast of how little work and how much drinking they do.

I conclude that many of our schools do a poor job of motivating their pupils to take English standards seriously, and are not teaching basic topics such as grammar, spelling and punctuation effectively. Above all, they are not correcting errors, so how are pupils to know what is right and what is wrong? I know that correction takes time, but if all teachers did it, the burden on each individual would be much reduced. One of my final-year home students told me that I was the only lecturer ever to have corrected her English, and that she was grateful for it, unlike some others. We need constructive criticism and correction from primary school onwards. We need to tell the country that good English matters.

(Lamb 2009)

Compare this passage with your own experience. Are there elements of this that you might agree with? Are there claims that seem over-stated or inaccurate?

Now read the following passage, from an article published in Greasley and Cassidy (2010) called 'When it Comes Round to Marking Assignments: How to Impress and How to "Distress" Lecturers'. This passage describes what impresses lecturers most and annoys them most when marking assignments:

Marking assignments

In this respect, we should also note the role of individual differences across markers who may have their own idiosyncratic sources of frustration, biases and expectations (Grainger, Purnell, and Zipf 2008, Sadler 2005). For example, some tutors may place a higher value on presentation, language and attention to details, whereas other marks may view this as 'style over substance', pointing out that the content is what matters most. These individual biases may also depend on guide lines and instruction presented in the context of a course, e.g. if the tutor has emphasised particular aspects of presentation in the lectures, failing to adhere to these guidelines may have a disproportionate impact on the relevant marking criteria (my own personal 'pet hate' is failing to number and head tables – despite this being emphasised in lectures).

(Greasley and Cassidy 2010: 180)

Does this passage suggest new areas of criticism of the previous passage, or does it reinforce some doubts that you had raised, based on your own experience and reflection? While you might feel better if you had already thought of the issues that Greasley and Cassidy raise, both increasing knowledge and personal reflection are necessary to improve critical thinking. As Taylor points out, he did not recognise that what he was being taught and what he came to believe contradicted his own experience until he read Chomsky's critical review of a book written by a behaviourist.

TOO DESCRIPTIVE!

One of the most common complaints of academics is that students' work is too descriptive, that it repeats what a source said rather than analysing the source and making a judgement. The judgement needs to be supported by evidence, but academics expect students to look at the evidence (read widely), balance and question the evidence, and then form an opinion.

Too often, students summarise sources or, worse, just quote, and expect that to be understood as evidence in itself. When you write an assignment, you tell a story. Within that story, what other people have said can contribute information, evidence or support, but you must keep the focus on your own story.

EXAMPLES OF CRITICAL THINKING
Sample assignment 1

Read the following passage (Sample assignment 1) from a student assignment, that answers the question, '"Soft power is not just a matter of ephemeral popularity." To what extent has soft power replaced hard power as the best means of achieving desired outcomes in International Relations?' This assignment begins with a definition from Nye (2004: 2) that suggests the meanings of both hard and soft power. This definition states that power is 'the ability to influence the behaviour of others to get the outcomes one wants... You can coerce them with threats; you can induce them with payments; or you can attract and co-opt them to want what you want.' The writer then goes on to develop his answer.

Sample assignment 1

This essay will look at the two theories of hard and soft power and will explain the changes in the nature of power through the years, and look at how soft power has become more important in international relations in the twenty-first century.

First, this essay will look at the concept of hard power. The historian A.J.P. Taylor stated that 'the test of a Great Power is... the test of strength for war' (Nye 1990b: 54). Nye also created a chessboard theory in relation to the different types of power. The chessboard theory gives power three dimensions. The top board relates to hard military power. Nye suggests that the United States is the only superpower with the military might over the rest of the world. This would mean that we are living in a uni-polar world. However, there are other dimensions to consider for global power in the twenty-first century such as economic issues or transnational issues (Nye 2004a: 4).

The historian Walter Russell Mead splits hard power into economic power and military power, as did Nye, but Mead renames them sticky power and sharp power. Sharp power, being military might is at the centre of the American system. Militarily, the United States have two hundred and fifty thousand troops in Asia, Europe and the Middle East. The United States also has the world's largest intelligence agencies which provides them with information from anywhere on the globe. Mead's view is that if a country, such as the United States has such high military supremacy and is consequently almost impossible to beat, other countries will stop trying to beat them. This would give the United States increased power over all others as they cannot beat the United States (Mead 2004a: 25–29).

Sticky power, being economic power is based on encouraging others through trade. Once economic trade has started between the two parties, the party is almost stuck by dependency for economic prosperity. Mead sees the sticky power as theoretically able to prevent war through economic dependency.

As you read sample assignment 1, look at how the writer uses his sources. Keep in mind – as the marker will – whether the writer is addressing the question of the extent to which 'soft power [has] replaced hard power as the best means of achieving desired outcomes'. Does the writer critically analyse the concepts of soft and hard power, or does he describe other people's ideas about these concepts?

After a signposting or organising paragraph ('This essay will look at the two theories') that sets out what he intends to do, the writer introduces a quotation from Taylor that underlines the previous definition of hard power. However, the quote is not mentioned further; instead, the writer goes on to discuss Nye's 'chess-board theory'. The writer mentions its three dimensions of military, economic and transnational issues. Next, he turns to another theory rather than developing his discussion of the chessboard theory further. The theory that he turns his attention to, Mead's theory of 'sharp' and 'sticky' power, is not identified as the second theory mentioned in the first paragraph. This failure to identify the theory clearly weakens the comparison. The writer then gives examples of the sharp power of the United States and, in the next paragraph, he discusses how sticky power differs from sharp power.

However, he does not contrast or directly compare Nye's theory, of three parts, with Mead's theory, which seems to have two parts. Nye's and Mead's theories seem to overlap, but neither the **similarities** nor the **differences** are highlighted in this discussion. This descriptive writing does not critically analyse its sources.

Sample assignment 2

A more successful approach to handling sources can be seen in the following passage (Sample assignment 2), in which the writer compares two theories which describe how children learn to read. This passage is a more successful example of critical thinking. The writer describes Firth's stage theory clearly. Then she turns to a competing theory, introducing Ehri's theory with the phrase, 'some researchers have criticised Firth's stage theory'. This aligns the student writer with Ehri, listing the issues that distinguish Ehri's theory from Firth's earlier conceptualisation of the process of learning to read.

Sample assignment 2

In addition to the strategies used in early reading, the stages of reading development have also been widely researched. Frith (1985) proposes three stages for reading development. The first one he describes is the 'logographic' stage. The child is able to recognise words by looking at the prominent features of the word; they rely on visual cues, this may be a letter of their name for example. Therefore they are unable to read new words or non-words at this stage.

The second stage is 'alphabetic'; the child learns to read by considering grapheme-phoneme correspondences, in other words they start to associate letters with sounds. The final stage is the 'orthographic' stage; the child is able to recognise whole words and therefore has developed an adult like reading system (Harley 2008).

However, some researchers have criticised Frith's stage theory of reading development for being too general. Ehri (1992) proposes four phases of reading development and illustrates several ways in which it differs from Frith's (1985) stage theory. First, she prefers the term 'phase' in regards to describing reading development, in contrast to the term 'stage' that Frith uses. She states that the use of the word 'stage' gives the implication that each stage is a prerequisite to the next, 'stages are discrete, non-overlapping periods of development' (Ehri 1999: 83).

A second difference is that Frith's stage theory is centred around the general development of reading whereas Ehri's phases of development focus on the development of sight word reading (Ehri 1999). A final criticism is of the use of terms Frith chooses to use. She claims that the term 'logographic' is somewhat misleading. English children don't remember the 'unified wholes' of the visual forms of words like the Chinese logographic or orthography. Instead they remember selected cues to recognise words (Ehri 1999).

(From Gemma Chaplin)

When comparing theories, approaches or discussions, be explicit about the points of comparison. Limit your description to the most important issues. Assignments and dissertations are written against word limits (professional academic texts, such as journal articles, are too). In the word allotment that you are given, you must tell your story, rather than repeat your source's ideas. That means that you may need to sketch out broad areas of agreement and then discuss the specific points of disagreement. Remember, too, that even if you've written something, you can cut it out. If you find that you do not have enough space within the word limit to discuss important points, go back over the text that you've written and look for examples and particularly extended quotations that can be dropped.

Sample assignment 3

Sample assignment 3 (overleaf) shows another extract in which the writer discusses the development of the concept of insider trading. The writer gives a great deal of information about the criminal prosecution of the traders. Much of this information could be reduced or eliminated to focus on the increasing use of insider trading prosecution, and the difficulties of obtaining convictions for insider trading.

In this assignment, the descriptions of the outcomes of the convictions ('12-month suspended sentence', 'four defendants were each charged') provide illustration

---

Sample assignment 3

The first successful conviction for insider dealing in the UK, once it became illegal in 1980, was the 1987 case against Geoffrey Collier, one of London's top investment bankers and the former head of securities at Morgan Grenfell. 'Collier was given a 12-month suspended sentence and was fined £25,000 with £7,000 costs at the High Court in London.'[5] The high profile of this case gave a warning to others; the successful prosecution of such a well known face within London and the Stock Exchange proved to others that illegal practices will not be tolerated.

An example of an insider dealing case that failed was in 2004 was the Richard Spearmen case; this was due to an undecided jury, demonstrating just how complex and difficult these cases can be to prove. This case then underwent a retrial 2005. Eventually a successful conviction was secured; he was convicted of insider dealing along with three other defendants:

> The four defendants were each charged with a single count of conspiracy to contravene the provisions of section 52 of the Criminal Justice Act 1993 contrary to section 1 of the Criminal Law Act 1997.[6]

In particular it was charged against them that between 1 June 1997 and 28 April 2001, they conspired together and with others to deal on the London Stock Exchange. They were sentenced to 30 months' imprisonment and fined £169,000.[7]

---

and precision, backing up the claim that 'illegal practices will not be tolerated'. However, the details of the *Spearman* case ('the four defendants') do not support the important claim that obtaining convictions in insider trading cases is difficult. The description of the outcome of the case takes 75 words, which might better have been used to advance the claim that it is difficult to secure convictions for insider trading.

These three examples of student assignments demonstrate critical thinking skills with varying degrees of success, and they should help you to think about ways of improving your own academic writing. These examples have shown that it is clear to readers when writers are confused, so take the time to think about your response to the literature and the task you have been set. Plan your writing and revise it carefully to avoid some of the issues discussed here.

WHERE DO YOU STAND? STANCE IN ACADEMIC WRITING

We have emphasised the importance of making informed judgements as part of critical thinking and writing. In their discussion of the aspects of student assignments that impress lecturers, Greasley and Cassidy (2010) point out that one of the most important aspects is the writer's voice. They discuss:

> Presence of voice – a sense that the author has a 'political' stance or indeed conviction. This comes through in the way arguments are constructed but also how evidence has been gathered, presented, interrogated and then evaluated.
>
> (Greasley and Cassidy 2010: 182)

They note that not every discipline expects this sort of engagement, but essays that convey a sense of the writer's personal investment in the topic are usually considered to be strong.

This does not mean that you should foreground yourself in your writing. Academics have varying ideas about the use of personal pronouns (I, me, mine and we, us, our) based on the practices of their discipline. Some academics accept their use, whilst others feel that they are inappropriate in academic writing (Hyland 2002). However, in almost every area, academic texts are expected to focus on the topic, whether it is research or background sources, rather than on the writer.

However, writers are expected to engage with the topic in a clear and straightforward way, and this sense of engagement is created by the writer's stance. In a famous example, Watson and Crick's initial description of the structure of DNA, the authors use 'we' to announce their topic, but maintain their focus on their research findings, which they highlight with strongly evaluative words and phrases (underlined). These words and phrases signal the authors' stance:

Focusing on findings

We wish to suggest a structure for the salt of deoxyribose nucleic acid (D. N. A.). This structure has <u>novel</u> features which are <u>of considerable biological interest</u>.

(Watson and Crick 1953: 737)

A writer's stance shows where that person stands on a topic. As you read scholarly sources you should ask yourself whether the writers have a positive or negative stance towards their topics, or whether they find both strengths and weaknesses in the issue they are discussing. Assignments which lack a clear stance tend to be seen as too descriptive.

Sample assignment 4

Sample assignment 4, from a law assignment, demonstrates a clear stance.

Sample assignment 4

As a general rule, in English criminal law, opinion evidence is inadmissible. It is necessary to discuss the rationale behind this general rule in order to identify any possible exceptions and the reason as to why these exceptions have arisen.

In **DPP v Kilbourne**[1] it was stated by Lord Simon of Glaisdale that 'Evidence is admissible if it may be lawfully adduced at trial.' Therefore, some types of evidence, such as opinion evidence, may be legally relevant but not placed before the tribunal of fact due to the exclusionary rules regarding admissibility. This is illustrated in **Corke v Corke and Cook**[1] where it was stated by Sellers L. J. that 'Evidence is not a matter of mere logic. Evidence which is hearsay might well be relevant to the issues and of probative value but it is excluded and is inadmissible for practical consideration.' This theory can be applied to the inadmissibility of opinion evidence and provides logical reasoning as to why the general rule was established, as there is an indication that even though opinions may be relevant, they may be excluded due to practicality or unreliability.

It could be argued that opinion evidence is inadmissible as it is the role of the court to form opinions. Therefore, allowing witnesses to provide opinions could overshadow the primary function of the tribunal of fact, indicating the importance of upholding the general rule.

(From Sarah Mills)

This writer briskly sets out her topic, the admissibility of opinion in criminal law. She provides sources which confirm the general rule and begins to lay the groundwork for her true topic, 'possible exceptions and the reason as to why these exceptions have arisen'. This writer is in charge of her topic. She is telling her story, about the occasions when opinion may be admissible in court, rather than letting her sources tell their stories.

As you write, you need to use the linguistic tools that establish your stance. These tools indicate your opinion, whether strong agreement, strong disagreement, or a position between these poles. Some words and phrases that can be used to establish your stance include those listed in Table 3.2.

As you can see in Table 3.2, English has a wide variety of words that can be used to create an author's stance. Opposite is an extract from an article published in 2009 by Bartram and Bailey called 'Different Students, Same Difference?: A Comparison of UK and International Students' Understandings of 'Effective Teaching'. The signal phrases (underlined) indicate the authors' stance.

As you read 'The author's stance' notice how the writers, after offering what is – for professional academic writing – fairly strong criticism, use a phrase, 'it could be argued' which is quite indirect. They avoid writing, 'we argue', instead softening the criticism to 'it could be argued'. This type of balancing is characteristic of successful academic writing, in which writers use critical analysis to make judgements but convey these judgements in a carefully balanced manner.

Introductory verbs	seem, indicate, suggest
Thinking verbs	believe, assume, suggest
Reporting verbs	claim, find, confirm, assert
Modal verbs	will, may, might, could
Evaluative adjectives	important, misguided, wrong, inaccurate, limited
Modal adjectives	certain, definite
Evaluative adverbs	accurately, unsatisfactorily
Adverbs of frequency	often, sometimes
Modal adverbs	certainly, definitely
Modal nouns	assumption, possibility
Signalling words	furthermore, similarly

Table 3.2 **Taking a stance as an academic writer**

The author's stance

The notion of effective teaching has received much attention in recent years, though much of this has tended to focus more on schools than higher education. Some authors (Evans and Abbott, 1998; Patrick and Smart, 1998) link this lesser focus on effective university teaching to the absence of agreement on what this notion actually represents in a sector that lacks a unified view of its purpose. One view is that teacher effectiveness in HE can best be understood in the context of student success demonstrated via assessment. Campbell *et al.* (2004) and Berliner (2005) discuss the use of such outcomes-based indicators as a gauge for describing effectiveness and, <u>though such approaches are not without merit</u>, it could be argued that there is more to teacher effectiveness than supporting students in examination success, and that this might well be at odds with students' own subjective evaluations of teaching. In this regard, Yates (2005) draws a distinction between 'the effective teacher', as demonstrated by an analysis of student outcomes, and 'the good teacher' who arouses positive affective reactions in students.

(Bartram and Bailey 2009: 173)

SUMMARY

This chapter has examined how to build upon existing scholarship by engaging in active reading and critical academic writing. It has offered four examples of critical thinking in action in order to help you avoid making mistakes. The most important points in this chapter are that you should try not to be too descriptive in your academic writing, and that you should build upon the sources you read to communicate your own stance as you write.

The main arguments in this chapter were:

- Be an active reader
- Try to think outside the box
- Avoid giving too much description in your academic writing
- Engage in critique as you write about your sources
- Identify your own stance as a writer.

References

Bartram, B. and Bailey, C. (2009) Different Students, Same Difference?: A Comparison of UK and International Students' Understandings of 'Effective Teaching'. *Active Learning in Higher Education* 10: 172–184.

Greasley, P., and Cassidy, A. (2010) When it Comes Round to Marking Assignments: How to Impress and How to 'Distress' Lecturers. *Assessment and Evaluation in Higher Education* 35: 173–189.

Hyland, K. (2002) Authority and Invisibility: Authorial Identity in Academic Writing. *Journal of Pragmatics* 34: 1091–1112.

Lamb, B. (2009) British Undergraduates Make Three Times as Many Errors in English as Do Ones from Overseas. *Quest*, unpaginated.

Nye, J. S., Jr (2004) *Soft Power: The Means to Success in World Politics*. New York: Public Affairs.

Taylor, L. (2010) Thinking Outside the Box. *The Times Higher Education* 11 March 2010: 43–45.

Watson, J. D. and Crick, F. H. C. (1953) Molecular Structure of Nucleic Acids. *Nature* 171: 737–738.

PART 2

PLANNING

Planning your academic writing is a crucial part of effective critical thinking. As previously mentioned, criticality requires you to develop your own position on a topic and gather the evidence to persuade your audience that this stance is valid. The key to successful planning is skill in time management, but this can take some practice as you juggle many commitments at once.

- Try to improve your time management skills
- Think about the demands of each research project
- Manage your academic and extra-curricular commitments
- Give yourself sufficient thinking time to develop innovative approaches and ideas.

4 ▶ COMPONENTS OF CRITICAL THINKING

This chapter investigates some of the key components of critical thinking and analysis. It offers tips on making connections as you read and write, developing reflectivity, and becoming more independent as a scholar. The chapter emphasises the importance of effective time management and the value of long-term planning to help you achieve your academic and professional goals.

This chapter covers:

- Components of critical thinking in academia
  - Connections
  - Reflectivity
  - Independence
  - Time management
  - Intellectual development
  - Context
  - Analysis
  - Long-term planning.

Using this chapter

Topic	Page
Components of critical thinking in academia	44
Connections	45
Reflectivity	46
Independence	47
Time management	48
Intellectual development	48
Context	49
Analysis	49
Long-term planning	50

INTRODUCTION

This chapter explores some of the key components of critical thinking in academic contexts in order to support you in planning your research and writing at university. One of the best ways to become a more effective critical thinker is to organise your time to give yourself space for reflection. By suggesting some of the main aspects of adopting a more analytic approach, this chapter offers you some tools to trial as you work towards improving your academic performance.

COMPONENTS OF CRITICAL THINKING IN ACADEMIA

This chapter explores eight important components of critical thinking which are particularly relevant for your development as a scholar, but there are multitudes of other issues which could be considered, and as you think in more depth about ways of working effectively you will identify many more. Here are eight essential aspects of criticality you should consider for advanced-level study:

Critical thinking

1 **Connections**

2 **Reflectivity**

3 **Independence**

4 **Time management**

5 **Intellectual development**

6 **Context**

7 **Analysis**

8 **Long-term planning.**

Although these components are represented here as a numbered list, you will call upon the various skills they entail at different times and often simultaneously, so you should not think about them in a linear way. For instance, as you are planning for the long term by considering your career options, you may engage in reflectivity to analyse your personal strengths, experiences and preferences in the light of the professional opportunities you identify. At the same time, you may be making connections between the expertise you are developing in academia and the require-ments of the professional context you are interested in so that you can present yourself as a strong candidate when you apply for jobs. In addition, you may demonstrate independence as you take practical steps to achieve your personal and professional goals. Figure 4.1 (opposite) illustrates the inter-connectivity of these eight components of critical thinking:

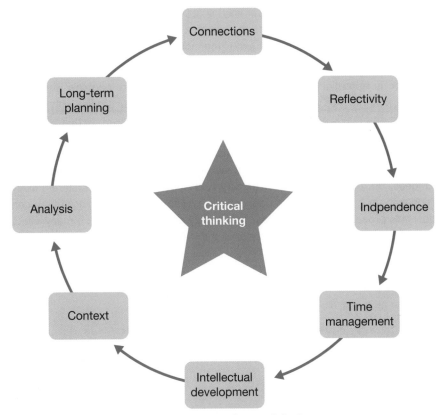

Figure 4.1 **Inter-connected components of critical thinking**

<u>C</u>onnections

Critical thinking is creative thinking, and it relies upon being able to identify useful links and implications that other people have missed. In particular, it involves being able to make connections between these three areas:

■ The ideas you encounter

■ The information you have already acquired

■ A task you have to undertake.

Critical thinking involves innovation and, by critiquing other people's ideas, you can make a contribution to knowledge in your subject area, yet this does not necessarily involve producing a radically new hypothesis. As an academic writer, you can offer new insights within your specialist area by bringing together information that has not previously been linked to identify new connections and their significance.

For instance, you might use a neglected theoretical perspective to reassess a subject you are researching and writing about. Using a theory associated with one area in another context is a practical way of making a contribution to your field by revealing fresh perspectives. Another practical way to apply your critical thinking and thus contribute to developing knowledge in your area would be to focus on a specific topic. The narrower your focus as a writer, the more you can go into depth, and the more likely you are to come up with ideas that no-one else has discovered.

Discussion is essential to seeing connections between other people's ideas and your own, so try to give yourself opportunities to talk about your studies with friends, colleagues and family members. Reading widely can also help you to perceive links between ideas. However, if you do not manage your time so that you have space to read and discuss your projects, you may become stressed and this will inhibit your ability to see sufficiently clearly to identify connections between concepts, data and ideas. So, effective time management and opportunities for debate are likely to enhance your ability to make connections, whilst stress and a lack of time can hinder this process. Figure 4.2 gives a summary of the factors which many affect your ability to make connections as a critical thinker in academia.

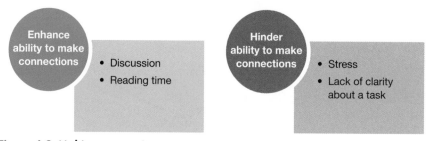

Figure 4.2 **Making connections**

Reflectivity

The best way to perceive new links between ideas is to develop your ability to reflect upon issues in depth. Not everyone is naturally reflective, but it is possible to strengthen this ability with practice. Reflection involves looking back over events and experiences to learn about your own strengths and weaknesses, then applying these lessons to your future actions.

Reflective practice is distinctive in each disciplinary and professional context, so you should investigate the specific requirements in your own discipline. If you are given assignments which involve reflective writing it is particularly important to familiarise yourself with the conventions in your subject area, and you should check with your tutors if you are unsure. Reflective writing is different to academic writing because it is personal, whereas academic writing is usually more formal and, although viewpoints are also expressed, these tend to be articulated in more scholarly ways than in reflective writing.

It is helpful to have clear guidelines when you engage in reflective practice for academic or professional purposes, and these can help you apply your insights to future actions. Reflection is most effective when it impacts upon your behaviour in positive ways, but can be hindered if you are unable to see the bigger picture or relate theories to your practice. To help yourself develop reflectivity you can read about models of reflection or ask your tutors for advice. If your university provides support in personal development planning, you can also seek help in developing this aspect of critical thinking. Figure 4.3 gives a summary of the factors which many affect your capacity for reflectivity in academia.

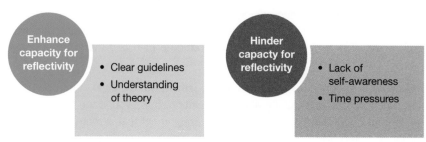

Figure 4.3 **Reflectivity**

Independence

Critical thinking at university involves taking a stance on the issues you are studying and making your mark as a researcher and writer. Tutors are often impressed by well-argued assignments which are innovative and engage with the issues in a fresh way. To achieve this in your own academic work, you should adhere to the guidelines you are given and try to develop confidence as a scholar in your own right.

The more familiar you are with the conventions in your discipline, the more confident you can be in experimenting with ways of articulating your own ideas. Reading the texts your tutors recommend and exploring beyond this literature will help you to identify successful models of communication and adapt these to become a more independent and critical thinker. On the other hand, if you are not sure about the common and acceptable forms of expression in your discipline, it will be harder to express your own ideas with clarity and force. Figure 4.4 gives a summary of the factors which many affect your ability to demonstrate independence in academia.

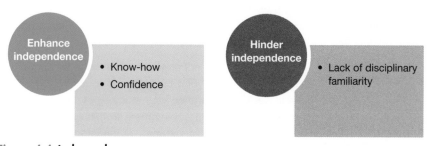

Figure 4.4 **Independence**

Time management

The process of thinking critically is extremely time-consuming, so the sooner you get started on an academic project, the better your chances of demonstrating criticality will be. Time management involves planning both on a macro level and on a micro level. In terms of macro level planning, you might consider the demands of a course you are studying and the deadlines for written assessments, so you know when you are likely to be most busy with academic work and you can organise your other commitments accordingly. In terms of micro level planning, you might consider how to write an individual assignment in good time by working backwards from the deadline and making sure you produce a plan and then a draft, leaving plenty of time to revise and edit your writing.

Judgement is essential for good time management; for example, it can be hard to know when to stop researching and begin writing, but if you judge this wrong you may run out of time and have to submit an assignment that is more of a draft than a properly edited piece of work, and that can never do you credit as an academic writer. If you tend to have poor personal organisation, be aware that this an area you need to work on and think about macro and micro level planning for your academic work before taking on too many extra-curricular commitments. Figure 4.5 gives a summary of the factors which many affect your ability to manage your time effectively in academia.

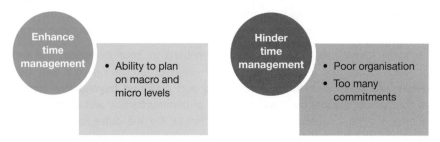

Figure 4.5 **Time management**

Intellectual development

By studying your chosen subject at an advanced level, you are giving yourself the best chance of promoting your own intellectual development. You are likely to develop intellectually if you read widely, and to do this you need to learn how to research effectively and evaluate the materials you find, as discussed in Part One.

To engage with the key theories in your subject area you will need to be committed to your studies and prepared to research beyond the materials you are given in your lectures. You will also have to seek to strengthen your study skills, and by reading this book you have already shown excellent commitment to this essential aspect of intellectual development. Figure 4.6 gives a summary of the factors which many affect your intellectual development.

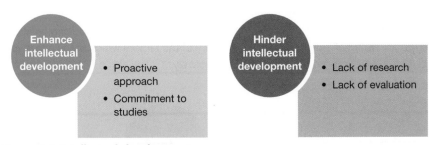

Figure 4.6 **Intellectual development**

Context

Strong critical thinkers are often good at assessing the context when they are reading a source or debating an issue. This can include an awareness of the audience, bias and hidden assumptions when evaluating texts or engaging in discussion. To do this you might draw on your general knowledge, your experience, and your understanding of the theoretical literature in your subject area.

To increase your awareness of relevant contexts for your studies, you can follow current affairs and keep good records of the sources you read, so you can refer back to key texts as they become relevant for a particular assignment. Your tutors provide essential contextual information for your assessments in lectures and other classes, so maximise your chances of academic success by attending, taking clear notes, and participating fully. Figure 4.7 gives a summary of the factors which many affect your awareness of the contexts which are relevant to your studies.

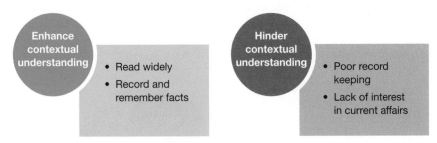

Figure 4.7 **Context**

Analysis

Analysis involves breaking down a subject into its constituent parts, examining these in depth, investigating how they inter-relate and assessing the implications for a particular purpose. Within academia you should employ skills of analysis to read sources closely and evaluate their strengths and weaknesses for your purpose as a writer.

The analysis of texts relies on an ability to skim read and scan sources effectively. It requires you to read with a critical eye and exercise doubt both about the sources you read and concerning your own perspective. This takes time and concentration, so be prepared to commit yourself to intensive research before producing your own academic writing. Figure 4.8 gives a summary of the factors which many affect your ability to analyse information and ideas effectively.

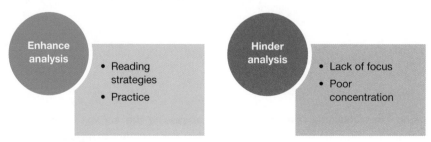

Figure 4.8 **Analysis**

Long-term planning

Effective critical thinking can help you to identify personal, academic and professional aims and work towards achieving them. Critical thinking is also essential in judging when to revise your goals or the methods you are adopting to pursue them.

Long-term planning does not guarantee that you will achieve everything to set out to do, but taking the actions that your plans imply dramatically increases the likelihood that you will. The key to fulfilling your long-term plans is to identify objectives which will incrementally take you closer towards your target. For instance, if you aim to obtain a first class degree, you could concentrate on obtaining an excellent grade for a specific assessment, which will take you a step closer to your ambition. Figure 4.9 gives a summary of the factors which many affect your ability to plan for the long term.

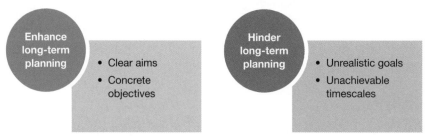

Figure 4.9 **Long-term planning**

SUMMARY

To summarise, if you cultivate your skills as a critical thinker you can reduce the confusion in your life and become a more committed and confident scholar, as Figure 4.10 suggests.

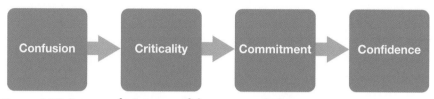

Figure 4.10 **From confusion to confidence as a scholar**

The main arguments in this chapter were:

- The ability to perceive connections between issues and ideas is vital to critical thinking
- A capacity for reflectivity is crucial for critical thinking
- Independence is a key part of critical thinking
- Time management is fundamental to successful critical thinking
- Fostering your own intellectual development is an essential part of critical thinking
- Awareness of contexts is important in critical thinking
- Effective analysis of texts underpins critical thinking
- Long-term planning is facilitated by strong critical thinking.

5 ▶ A STRATEGY FOR ANALYSIS

This chapter explores a strategy for analysis adapted from the philosophical writings of Descartes (1596–1650). The purpose of offering this strategy is not to determine your own approach to critical thinking, but to offer some suggestions with which you can experiment to develop your own style of analysis. The chapter discusses ways to avoid errors of understanding and academic practice, to help equip you for success in academia.

This chapter covers:

- Generating disciplinary knowledge
- Using your judgement in academia
- Descartes' critical thinking method
- Errors of understanding
- Errors of academic practice
- Applications of Descartes' theories.

Using this chapter

Topic	Page
Generating disciplinary knowledge	54
Using your judgement in academia	55
Descartes' critical thinking method	55
Errors of understanding	56
Errors of academic practice	57
Applications of Descartes' theories	57
Doubt everything	57
Examine other people's ideas	58
Scepticism is useful	59
Critique your own ideas	59
Analyse texts	60
Revise your writing	60
Talk about your ideas	60
Edit your writing	60
See beyond the surface level	61

INTRODUCTION

One way to improve your critical thinking at university is to develop a method for organising your intellectual activity and communicating ideas in your written assessments. This chapter offers one approach to thinking and writing critically that you can adapt and apply to your own academic projects based on your personality and preferences. There are many other ways of strengthening your skills of analysis, and you will probably need to trial a range of strategies before you settle on the most effective for you.

You may find it useful to revise your approach to critical thinking for specific projects, for instance, a dissertation involves extended research and writing, and extended projects are likely to demand a different kind of analysis to many of the assignments you have encountered before. As you progress to new levels of study or move into professional contexts you can develop your analytic method and strengthen your ability to communicate ideas to others.

GENERATING DISCIPLINARY KNOWLEDGE

At university one of your core activities is generating knowledge about the subject you have chosen to study. Initially, you will pursue your own intellectual development, but as you develop skill as a researcher and writer, you can contribute to your academic community by evaluating theories and seeing issues in a new light. By building on this expertise you will also help to shape your chosen professional context.

While you are studying, disciplinary knowledge is important if you are to perform well. For example, many academic assessments are designed to support your acquisition of specialist knowledge, and to ensure you develop as a specialist in your field your tutors use marking criteria to test your knowledge. Take advantage of any opportunities you have to discuss with your tutors the key concepts you are expected to master, and attend your lectures and other classes regularly, so you do not miss out on any essential information.

As you develop a more systematic approach to finding, interpreting and using data within academia, you will give yourself the best chance of contributing to the development of knowledge in your subject area. One way to do this is to critique existing research and practice, but to do so you need to establish a good grounding in the fundamentals of your discipline, which includes an awareness of the most influential scholars, the main theoretical approaches, and some of the currently controversial issues. Obviously, the basics you need to acquire depend upon your discipline, and it is up to you to find out what your tutors expect you to know within each course. The intended learning outcomes for your courses are usually explained in handbooks or other course literature including online, but check with your tutors if you are unsure about the disciplinary knowledge they expect you to acquire.

USING YOUR JUDGEMENT IN ACADEMIA

However, you are unlikely to be successful at engaging with and contributing to the body of knowledge in your discipline if you cannot distinguish between accurate research and convincing arguments on one hand, and inaccurate or misleading information on the other. To think critically about the ideas other people present, you need to exercise your academic judgement throughout the process of researching and writing for assessment. Here are six ways in which judgement is important for academic work:

Judgement in academia

- You need to judge what you need to do for a particular project or assessment
- You need to judge how to prioritise tasks to accomplish your projects within set timescales
- You need to judge which literature to read
- You need to judge which data to employ for your writing
- You need to judge what to argue in your writing
- You need to judge where to revise and edit your writing.

You can enhance your ability to make these six academic judgements by employing a method and, although this will not solve all the challenges you encounter as a scholar, a strategic approach may enhance your effectiveness as a researcher, thinker and writer.

DESCARTES' CRITICAL THINKING METHOD

The seventeenth-century French philosopher René Descartes (1596–1650) developed a method for critical thinking that has been relatively neglected by contemporary students in the British higher education system. Overleaf are nine applications of his philosophy which represent a strategy for strengthening your skills of analysis and boosting your academic performance.

Descartes wrote about his philosophical theories in the book, *Meditations on First Philosophy in which are demonstrated the Existence of God and the Distinction between the Human Soul and Body,* which was first published in Latin in 1641. As he introduces the *Meditations*, Descartes explains that he has been reflecting upon 'how I go about acquiring knowledge', and the ideas he articulates are also applicable to the process of generating disciplinary knowledge at university (1641: 3).

Descartes argues that we all have a capacity to generate knowledge, but that we have to train this ability in order to maximise our effectiveness as critical thinkers.

With this aim in mind, he proposes a method for avoiding two kinds of errors (1641: 18). Descartes describes these as errors of the intellect and of the will, but in terms of studying in contemporary academia we can view these two categories as errors of understanding and errors of academic practice.

Nine principles of critical thinking and analysis

1 **D**oubt everything

2 **E**xamine other people's ideas

3 **S**cepticism is useful

4 **C**ritique your own ideas

5 **A**nalyse texts

6 **R**evise your writing

7 **T**alk about your ideas

8 **E**dit your writing

9 **S**ee beyond the surface level.

ERRORS OF UNDERSTANDING

In terms of the nine-part strategy for strengthening your skills of analysis that is mentioned above, the following are ways of avoiding errors of understanding in your academic studies:

- Doubt everything
- Examine other people's ideas
- Scepticism is useful
- Critique your own ideas
- Analyse texts.

Overall, these five suggestions amount to being cautious as you encounter other people's ideas. When you read journal articles and other sources including material you have accessed online, remember that just because information has been published in some form, this does not mean that it is reliable. Taking everything you read on trust without analysing the contents can lead to some serious errors in understanding and, in terms of your academic work, this can cost you marks.

In fact, if an assignment contains errors in terms of the information it contains or the interpretation of key concepts, it is likely to fail. Similarly, if an assignment does not fulfil the brief because the writer has not understood the question or main task, this can also result in a fail. So, practising healthy scepticism as you undertake research and reading is invaluable for success at university.

ERRORS OF ACADEMIC PRACTICE

The following are ways of avoiding errors of academic practice:

- Revise your writing
- Talk about your ideas
- Edit your writing
- See beyond the surface level.

Academic practice means being scholarly as you generate and communicate your ideas at university, and these four suggestions will help you to achieve this. Descartes comments that it is not easy to sustain this kind of criticality, writing, 'this will be hard work' (1641: 3). He admits that when it comes to questioning both other people's ideas and his own, 'a kind of laziness pulls me back into my old ways' (1641: 3). Nevertheless, the effort you put into talking about your ideas, planning what to write, revising, and editing your writing will pay dividends when it comes to your academic performance. These five activities are fundamental to good academic practice, and they represent the path to enhancing your enjoyment of advanced-level study by helping you to manage the complexity of information and ideas you encounter as a specialist in your field.

APPLICATIONS OF DESCARTES' THEORIES

Figure 5.1 (overleaf) demonstrates all nine applications of Descartes' theories for research and writing at university. These nine suggestions for avoiding errors of understanding and academic practice are adapted not only from Descartes' *Meditations*, but also from his book, *Discourse on the Method of Rightly Conducting one's Reason and Seeking Truth in the Sciences* which was first published in 1637.

Doubt everything

Descartes argues that to acquire a firm foundation of knowledge it is necessary to reject any ideas that can be doubted, and in the *Discourse* he offers some basic rules of logic to guard against making errors of judgement. For instance, he determines 'never to accept anything as true if I didn't have evident knowledge of its truth: that is, carefully to avoid jumping to conclusions and preserving old opinions' (1636: 8).

It is easy to take some ideas for granted without interrogating their evidence base, especially our own opinions. This is partly because it would be very time-consuming to question everything we think and read; nevertheless, scholars who are good at critical thinking exercise doubt, and they seek solid evidence before accepting the ideas they encounter. As a researcher, you should interrogate the theories, information, and arguments presented by scholars in your field as well as being prepared

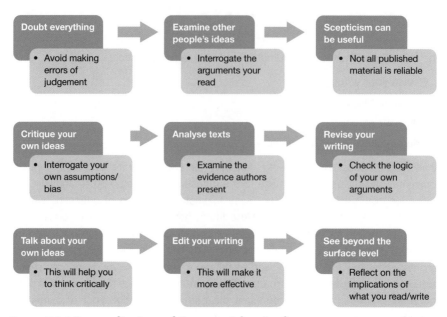

Figure 5.1 **Nine applications of Descartes' theories for contemporary academia**

to revise your own ideas. You can help yourself avoid making errors of judgement in your own academic work by applying Descartes' principle of doubt.

Examine other people's ideas

Descartes also observes in the *Discourse* that 'some men make mistakes in reasoning' and 'commit logical fallacies' (1636: 14). As a scholar you should interrogate the academic arguments you read in order to avoid repeating any mistakes in your own writing. In terms of a strategy for examining other people's ideas, you could ask yourself these six questions as you interrogate a source:

- Is the main point clear and convincing?
- Do the sub-points support this position?
- Are the points backed up with evidence?
- Is the evidence convincing, relevant and complete?
- Is the evidence interpreted appropriately?
- Are the conclusions supported by the rest of the source?

You will think of additional questions which are particularly pertinent for your own reading as you interrogate the ideas authors present and, with practice, your ability to analyse texts will improve.

Scepticism is useful

As already suggested, Descartes advocates a method of enquiry based upon scepticism, which means analysing information for yourself before accepting it as true. As a scholar you can test the sources you read in these four ways:

- Check the authors' credentials – are they qualified or experienced in the subject area?
- Check other similar texts – do the facts/arguments corroborate your sources?
- Check the logic – are you convinced based on your own knowledge and instincts?
- Check with your peers – do other people find the sources unconvincing?

These are not the only questions to pose as you test the validity of your sources, but they are essential points to consider which will help you to cultivate a healthy scepticism whilst keeping an open mind as you research and write at university.

Critique your own ideas

As a scholar it is good practice to be aware of the limitations regarding your own thoughts and approaches because as Descartes comments in the *Discourse*, 'our convictions come much more from custom and example than from any certain knowledge' (1636: 7). We all make assumptions, and as academic writers we cannot avoid bias, but being aware of this is crucial to overcoming the distorting effects of bias upon our thinking.

Whilst you should not be negative or dismissive of your own thoughts, you should also avoid pursuing your first ideas without taking the time to check their validity and build up an informed position. Following a method of enquiry can help you to do this, as Descartes explains in the *Discourse*. He expresses a desire to 'direct my thoughts in an orderly manner', and does so 'by starting with the simplest and most easily known objects in order to move up gradually to knowledge of the most complex, and by stipulating some order even among objects that have no natural order of precedence' (1636: 9).

You can adopt this technique by beginning with the basics, for example, by making sure that you understand the meaning of any key terms you are dealing with as a researcher and writer. You might then move on to checking that you understand what your assignment brief or research question entails, and then to thinking about how you will respond, whilst thinking critically about the quality and relevance of your own response. A next step might be to make a plan and share it with a friend to help you critique the organisation of your ideas. After this, you could draft your piece of work, leaving sufficient time to revise and edit it.

Time is often the determining factor when it comes to being able to critique your own ideas effectively and, as Descartes remarks, 'those who go very slowly but always on the right path can make much greater progress than those who sprint and go astray' (1636: 1). This means that being organised is essential to success, and adopting a strategy for your critical thinking can help you to get organised as a scholar.

Analyse texts

Reading is central to critical thinking at university because well-written texts provide essential information and potential models of effective argumentation. As Descartes reflects, 'reading good books is like having a conversation with the most distinguished men' and women (1636: 3). However, as suggested above, without analysing the ideas in the texts you read, you may make fundamental errors when you draw on them in your writing.

Revise your writing

Although this is not a point made directly by Descartes, his recommendation of a method for critical thinking implies that you should adopt an incremental approach to communicating your ideas within your academic community. As you revise your work, look again at the assignment brief or research question you investigated and ensure that you have addressed this fully. Here are some points to consider as you revise your writing:

- Check that you have addressed your task fully
- Check that you have introduced your work clearly
- Check that you have organised your ideas effectively
- Check that you have provided evidence to support your claims
- Check that you have evaluated the evidence you use
- Check that you have concluded your work effectively.

Talk about your ideas

In the *Discourse*, Descartes considers how people can make the most of their intellectual capabilities, writing, 'it isn't enough to have a good mind; what matters most is using it well' (1636: 1). Although Descartes does not explicitly recommend discussing ideas, this is a recognised method of scholarly enquiry which you can exploit to develop your own critical thinking at university. By expressing your thoughts to peers who respond constructively and challenge your thinking in a friendly way, you can give yourself the best chance of using your mind well because this discussion will make it easier to see any weaknesses or gaps you had missed.

Edit your writing

Whilst Descartes does not explicitly consider editing texts, his emphasis on adopting a method for thinking implies the necessity for a methodological approach to communicating ideas. If you present your thoughts in an unprofessional manner it is unlikely that they will be well received, so, just as you should revise your writing with care, take the time to edit your work prior to submission or dissemination to members of your academic community. Here are some points to consider as you edit your writing:

- Check that your sentences flow and make sense
- Check that your paragraphs are clear and well developed
- Check that your sub-sections are organised consistently
- Check that your language is sufficiently formal
- Check that your spelling is accurate
- Check that your punctuation is accurate.

See beyond the surface level

Descartes offers a rule of logic in the *Discourse*, which is 'to make all my enumerations so complete, and my reviews so comprehensive, that I could be sure that I hadn't overlooked anything' (1636: 9). If you are systematic about your critical thinking you are more likely to see beyond a superficial level when you are researching and thinking about what to write.

You will improve with practice, as Descartes suggests in the *Discourse* with his remark, 'as I employed the method I felt my mind getting more and more into the habit of conceiving things sharply and clearly' (1636: 10). You may find that you surprise yourself with the extent of your intellectual innovation because, as Descartes suggests, by employing a method of enquiry, 'one man on his own is much more likely to hit upon such truths than a whole population is' (1636: 7).

SUMMARY

Following a method like this nine-step system for thinking and writing adapted from Descartes' *Meditations* and *Discourse* is not the only way to improve your criticality and confidence as a scholar. The main point of this chapter has been to recommend adopting a strategy rather than dictating the form that this should take. If you reflect upon and organise your own research and writing, you can make your mark in academia and enjoy doing so.

The main arguments in this chapter were:

- Do not take information or ideas at face value
- Critique your own ideas
- Revise and edit your writing.

References

Descartes, R. (1641) *Meditations on First Philosophy in which are demonstrated the Existence of God and the Distinction between the Human Soul and Body*. trans. by Jonathan Bennett (2007). Available from <http://www.earlymoderntexts.com/pdf/descmed.pdf> [6 April 2010].

Descartes, R. (1637) *Discourse on the Method of Rightly Conducting one's Reason and Seeking Truth in the Sciences*. trans. by Jonathan Bennett (2007). Available from <http://www.earlymoderntexts.com/pdf/descdisc.pdf> [6 April 2010].

PART 3

WRITING

Academic writing is an important way to communicate your
critical thinking at university. It requires you to develop a strong
awareness of the scholarly conventions in your discipline. You
should read widely with a critical eye to build up an awareness
of how professionals in your subject area articulate their ideas.
Crucially, you should allow yourself time to plan, revise and edit
your writing prior to submission.

- Read widely to identify effective models of scholarly writing
- Credit the authors by referencing clearly
- Discuss your ideas
- Plan your writing
- Revise your writing
- Edit your writing.

6 ▶ PREPARING TO WRITE

This chapter looks at academic assignments and investigates ways of analysing an assessment task. It considers how to select sources and preview them, for instance by skimming and scanning the contents. The chapter emphasises the different conventions of writing in disciplinary contexts and advises you to read journal articles in your subject area to become familiar with the culture of writing in your field.

This chapter covers:

- Academic assignments
- Analysing a task
- Locating and selecting sources
- Previewing sources
- Writing and disciplinary specificity
- Conducting research.

Using this chapter

Topic	Page
Academic assignments	66
Analysing a task	66
Locating and selecting sources	67
Previewing sources	68
Skimming	68
Scanning	68
Writing and disciplinary specificity	69
Conducting research	69
Why read journal articles to inform your writing?	69
Why persevere?	70
The structure of different journal articles	71
Referencing sources	72

INTRODUCTION

This chapter explores the various kinds of preparation you may need to undertake before producing academic writing. It focuses on the role of critical thinking in preparing to write, and introduces some of the kinds of analysis you may wish to undertake as you read scholarly sources and develop your own ideas.

ACADEMIC ASSIGNMENTS

Many of the written assessments you undertake at university depend upon your skills of critical thinking and analysis. This is partly because assignments and bigger projects require you to undertake research, which cannot be done effectively without critiquing a range of academic sources and developing your own ideas on a topic. Figure 6.1 sets out some of the ways in which researchers employ critical thinking as they collect, evaluate and deploy data in their academic writing.

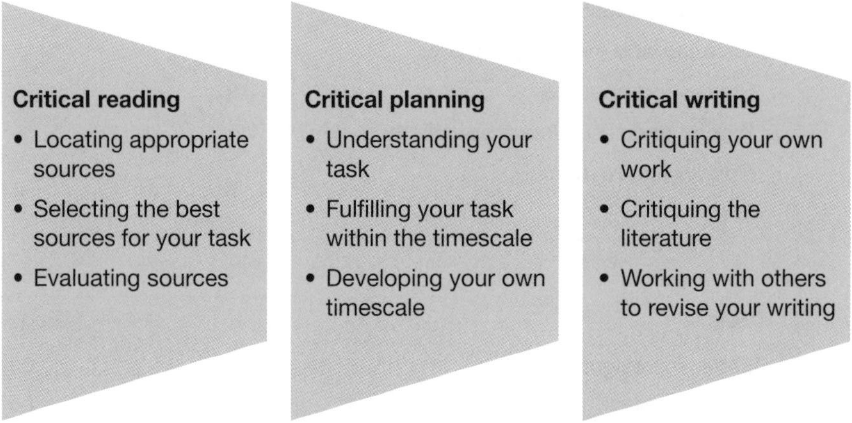

Critical reading

- Locating appropriate sources
- Selecting the best sources for your task
- Evaluating sources

Critical planning

- Understanding your task
- Fulfilling your task within the timescale
- Developing your own timescale

Critical writing

- Critiquing your own work
- Critiquing the literature
- Working with others to revise your writing

Figure 6.1 **Critical thinking for academic writing**

ANALYSING A TASK

If you are working on an assignment brief or set question, this is the first thing you need to read critically in order to identify what kind of information you require to respond in full, and to begin considering the position you will adopt. As you analyse your task or question, you may come up with an initial response, but you should not settle with this if you want to think about it critically. Sometimes a writer's first ideas are the best, but often further research reveals the early thoughts to be incomplete, and they are usually strengthened by taking time to read and reflect upon the topic.

Here are some questions you can ask yourself to analyse your task:

- What is the main point of the assessment or task?
- What are the criteria by which it will be assessed?
- What steps are required to complete it?
- How much time is needed to complete it?
- Which resources will be most useful?

LOCATING AND SELECTING SOURCES

Once you have analysed your task, the next stage is to locate appropriate sources to fulfil this brief. This involves skills of analysis as you search databases or other repositories for relevant sources. Check the titles of sources for key words which signal their relevance for your purpose, and consult the abstracts of journal articles to find out whether they cover your topic. As part of your critical approach to selecting sources you may consider the following 12 questions:

1 Who are the authors?
2 Are the authors authorities on their topic?
3 What is the topic?
4 Is the topic relevant to your task?
5 What is the main argument?
6 Is the main argument clear and convincing?
7 How reliable is the evidence?
8 Are there any gaps in the evidence?
9 Is the source up-to-date?
10 Is there a reason if it is not?
11 Is the source comprehensive?
12 Or is it too detailed for your purpose?

Keep a critical eye on the sources you are using because sometimes texts which initially appeared to be useful can turn out to be distractions. For instance, once you begin reading in earnest you might find the line of argument in a source hard to follow to the extent that it confuses you rather than clarifying the issues you are thinking about. Or, you may feel having read a few pages that a source does not deal with your topic as directly you first thought. You should trust your instincts and reject any source that does not seem to be helpful because your time could be better spent reading more appropriate material. The more you practise evaluating the relevance of your sources, the more adept at this you will become, so keep asking yourself whether your sources are appropriate as you read. On the other hand, it can be worth persevering with difficult material so you should not be too quick to reject challenging texts.

Here are some tips:

Rejecting sources

- Be prepared to reject sources you find confusing
- Trust your instincts if you feel a source is not useful for your task
- Distinguish between complex arguments and badly presented material (only reject the latter)
- Persevere with challenging texts which are well written.

PREVIEWING SOURCES

When you have located a range of potential sources for your research and selected the most appropriate texts, you should engage in another kind of critical thinking by previewing selected sources. You can deploy two techniques to evaluate the usefulness for your purpose, and these are **skimming** and **scanning**.

Skimming

This means reading relatively quickly to get an overview of a text. As you skim read you will discover the topic and scope of a source as well as the main argument and some of the themes. A useful skimming technique is to read the introduction, the conclusion, and the first sentence of each paragraph, known as the 'topic sentence'.

The topic sentence often articulates the point being made in a paragraph, so as you skim read you do not necessarily have to read the rest of the paragraph. If you were to read on, you may find that the rest of the paragraph contains evidence or an example to illustrate the point being made. You may also find that the rest of the paragraph contains an explanation of the issues raised by the topic sentence and, although you may skim over this, you should be aware that the explanation part of a paragraph is often where authors demonstrate their critical thinking by evaluating the evidence and articulating their own stance on the subject being discussed.

Scanning

This means concentrating on the sections in a text which are most relevant for your own purpose, and examining these in detail. Often readers skim a text to identify the main components, then scan the most relevant parts in more depth. As you scan you may be looking for data such as dates, statistics or historical facts in a source, or you might be most interested in the conclusions and recommendations made by researchers.

Whereas you could focus on the topic sentences in a source as you skim, you may wish to examine the evidence presented by authors when you scan in order to find the information you need to support your own academic writing. Scanning is most effective when you have a clear goal in mind as you read, such as looking for an author's stance on a topic, or learning about a particular theory you wish to write about.

WRITING AND DISCIPLINARY SPECIFICITY

At an advanced level, studying in your chosen field requires you to adopt distinctive conventions in your academic writing, which means that you should apply the general principles outlined in this book to your own field. As you undertake your degree studies you will be exposed to the common forms of communication in your discipline, which provide clues about the various ways scholars in your area generate and disseminate ideas. As you prepare for your career, you will also gain insight into the conventions for writing in your chosen professional context. In addition to exploring how successful scholars and professionals in your chosen area communicate ideas, be aware that everyone develops their own approach to academic writing. So, use the tips in this chapter to explore what works best for you.

CONDUCTING RESEARCH

As you undertake research, there are certain databases you should use to locate the most appropriate sources for your studies. The best place to learn about these is your university library, so you should find out about training courses or visit your subject librarian. You can use the relevant databases in your subject area to locate the journal articles that will provide the best information for your assignments. As journals contain up-to-date research in your area, they are essential for stimulating your critical thinking in response to your set assessments.

When you search for articles in your field you will encounter a vast amount of choice, so take the time to familiarise yourself with a small selection of journals at first. To get started, you could check out the reading lists your tutors provide and notice the names of a couple of journals. Start by looking at these journals to identify the themes they tend to include and the general format of the articles. Each journal has a mission, which you can read about in the hard copy or on the journal website. If you find it hard to remember the kinds of topics treated in the key journals in your field, you could make yourself a list with the title and stated aims of each publication. This will give you a head start when you are set an academic assignment that depends upon research and critical thinking.

Why read journal articles to inform your writing?

A potential benefit of reading scholarly articles is that they often represent strong examples of how critical thinking can be presented in a scholarly fashion, and this makes them possible models for your own academic writing. Within the relatively tight space of an article, researchers put forward a hypothesis or articulate a research question, and this acts as the trigger for the critical thinking that is displayed throughout the article. The authors of academic articles do not usually reveal their first thoughts on a subject, but before and during the writing process they incubate ideas and engage in extended critical thinking and discussion, so, what you read in an article is the authors' final assessment on their subject. As a reader you may be persuaded by their arguments based on evidence, or you may perceive weaknesses and wish to critique the article's contents.

Whether or not you are convinced by the argument in a journal article, you should appreciate the effort involved in producing scholarly writing and note that you cannot achieve the same level of professionalism without dedicating time to your academic writing. Scholarly authors research and plan their publications with care before drafting them in accordance with the culture of their discipline and the conventions of their target journal. Prior to publication, they submit their article to be sent for peer review by experts in their subject area, and these experts critique the contents and point out any limitations in the article. As a consequence, articles in peer reviewed journals are often superb examples of critical thinking presented in a scholarly format.

Why persevere?

As journal articles are written in an academic style and deal with specialist subjects, they can appear to be rather inaccessible if you are not accustomed to their style and format. Try not to be put off because scholarly writing gets easier to understand the more familiar you become with the conventions the authors employ. If you get an opportunity, you could ask your tutors for help in understanding articles, or enquire about relatively accessible articles to start with. Alternatively, you could work with a friend to read an article related to a subject you are studying, then discuss the main points and any parts you find difficult to understand. Reading one article on a topic can help to prepare you for reading others in a related area because authors often provide lots of information which gives you insight into the issues. You can pick up essential knowledge as you read by taking notes, and in a fairly short time you will build up a stronger appreciation of the topics you are studying.

It is well worth persevering with journal articles as sources to stimulate your critical thinking because they are written in a scholarly style and they can be exempla of how to present ideas within your academic community. Once you have learnt how to locate relevant articles, they can provide concise yet comprehensive information for your projects, and give you a real boost as you research and prepare to write. Without the focused, often expert accounts of relevant scholarship that journal articles provide, you might miss out on information that could help you develop your own innovative ideas. There are two main reasons why it pays to be able to locate appropriate journal articles and draw on them to enhance your academic writing:

Why read journal articles?

1 Scholarly articles are good examples of critical thinking

2 Scholarly articles are good examples of critical thinking in your discipline.

The structure of different journal articles

As mentioned above, scholarly articles are exempla of critical thinking within a specific subject area. The authors are experts in their field and have read widely in the relevant scholarly literature. Whilst it is not necessary for you to follow the conventions precisely because they are writing for publication and you should develop your own written style, it is important that you are familiar with the specialist vocabulary the authors use and the ways in which they present their research. For example, although it is not possible to generalise, in the **sciences** the following elements are often included in a scholarly journal article:

- Abstract
- Introduction
- Literature review
- Methodology
- Results
- Discussion
- Conclusions.

In contrast, in the humanities journal articles are often organised differently, and do not tend to report on the findings of an experiment. Although there is great variation and a wide range of types of publications, the following elements may be included in a scholarly journal article in the **humanities**:

- Abstract
- Introduction
- Literature review
- Main argument
- Supporting arguments
- Conclusion.

In the social sciences there are other structures, as discussed in the next chapter. As you are reading articles in your field you will notice common structures and components. However, be aware that as there is wide variation across the many kinds of journals, these two lists are only intended to give you a sense of the variety that exists.

Referencing sources

You need to reference your sources fully. Always make notes about the sources themselves as well as the content, so you can cite the author, date and page if you borrow ideas. You will also need to construct a complete list of references, and to do so you should follow the guidance your tutors provide about which referencing style to adopt. If you are unsure about any aspect of referencing, you should seek advice from your tutors or attend any training sessions offered at your university. If you are not aware of where to find support with your referencing, start by enquiring at your university library.

SUMMARY

This chapter has discussed various ways in which you can prepare to produce effective academic writing. It has emphasised the importance of critical reading in this preparation process, in particular the value of familiarising yourself with the conventions of scholarly writing in your subject area.

The main arguments in this chapter were:

- Select your sources with care
- Read your sources critically as your prepare to write
- Learn about the conventions of academic writing within your subject area.

SCHOLARLY WRITING

This chapter continues to examine the importance of journal articles as sources of specialist information and examples of academic writing in your subject area. The chapter considers the features of abstracts in journal articles and analyses a sample article in order to help you think critically about the research you read as you prepare to write.

This chapter covers:

- Journal article abstracts
- Key features of abstracts
- Key features of articles
- Analysis of a sample article.

Using this chapter

Topic	Page
Journal article abstracts	74
Key features of abstracts	75
Key features of articles	76
Analysis of a sample article	77
Introduction	77
Literature review	78
Method	79
Limitations	80
Results	81
Discussion	81
Conclusion	82
To sum up	82

INTRODUCTION

This chapter analyses a sample article about the effects of using information technology (IT) to conduct research. The article is written by Sarit Barzilai and Anat Zohar and it is called 'How Does Information Technology Shape Thinking?' This article was published in 2006 in the peer reviewed journal *Thinking Skills and Creativity* and, as an example of academic writing that has been reviewed by experts and published in an international journal, it provides insights into how you can present your critical thinking in a scholarly manner as you write.

Be aware that this article is in the field of educational research, and many of the conventions identified in this chapter are specific to that discipline, although some of these features are also common in other subject areas. For instance, in most peer reviewed journal articles the authors articulate the main argument clearly and offer a literature review to ground their discussion. As it would not be possible within the scope of this book to discuss articles from every subject area and this article deals with the subject of critical thinking, it is appropriate as an example for analysis.

As a scholar, you should be able to read any academic article on a relevant topic and analyse both the value and the limitations for your own studies. Try to think critically about the content and the structure of this sample article, and consider how the conventions differ from the articles your tutors have recommended to you.

JOURNAL ARTICLE ABSTRACTS

The role of the abstract of a journal article is to introduce the topic, main point, methods, and benefits of reading the article. There are often keywords listed at the end of the abstract which also provide clues to help potential readers decide whether an article is directly relevant to them. Opposite is the abstract for the article by Barzilai and Zohar called 'How Does Information Technology Shape Thinking?'

The keywords listed for this article include 'higher order thinking strategies', so it is appropriate as a source to support you in strengthening your skills of critical thinking and analysis. There are many different ways of writing an abstract, and it is important to remember that this example demonstrates only one approach. Being taken from the field of educational research, it falls into the general category of research in the social sciences, so it should not be applied unthinkingly to writing abstracts in the humanities or sciences.

Abstract

This study revisits a classic yet still intriguing question regarding information technology (IT): what difference does IT 'really' make, in terms of people's thinking? In order to explore this question, the effects of IT in authentic research settings were studied through retrospective interviews with 24 academic researchers. Analysis of the researchers' descriptions of their learning and thinking processes shows that the effects of IT on higher order thinking strategies can be classified, following Perkins (1985), into first order effects and second order effects. First order effects of IT amplify or improve existing thinking strategies, without changing their nature, while second order effects of IT cause significant changes in the researchers' thinking strategies. The results demonstrate that both types of effects take place in authentic research settings, often existing side by side. This article explores several examples of the ways in which IT affects higher order thinking strategies (such as forming research questions, constructing models and evaluating information), examines the types of effects created by IT, the conditions required for these effects to take place, and the role of distributed cognition.

Keywords: Higher order thinking strategies, cognitive effects of information technology, distributed cognition

(Barzilai and Zohar 2006: 130)

KEY FEATURES OF ABSTRACTS

There are some key features in this example which demonstrate the authors' agility as researchers and raise some issues for you to consider as you present your own ideas to a scholarly audience. As abstracts for scholarly articles usually provide a synopsis of the authors' main points they are like crystallised examples of critical thinking. This example is not necessarily intended to represent an ideal abstract, although it is very clear and informative. Notice that the authors identify the scope of their research, the main question they investigated, the literature they built upon as they explored the topic of critical thinking, and their findings. The key features of this abstract include:

Some features of a sample abstract from the social sciences

- Identification of the scope of the study
- Articulation of the research question
- Outline of methodology
- Reference to influential literature
- Definition of key terms
- Brief outline of results
- Suggestion of how research may be useful.

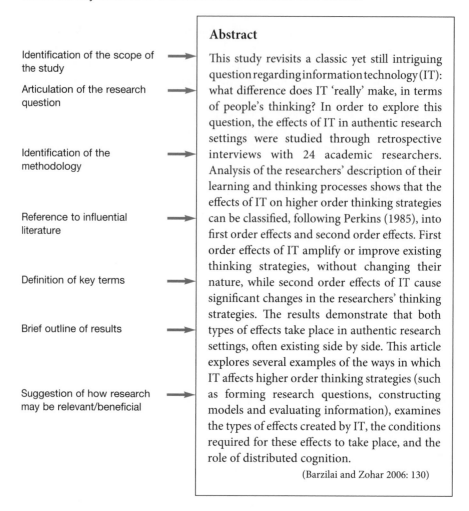

Below the key features of this abstract are identified with arrows:

Identification of the scope of the study

Articulation of the research question

Identification of the methodology

Reference to influential literature

Definition of key terms

Brief outline of results

Suggestion of how research may be relevant/beneficial

Abstract

This study revisits a classic yet still intriguing question regarding information technology (IT): what difference does IT 'really' make, in terms of people's thinking? In order to explore this question, the effects of IT in authentic research settings were studied through retrospective interviews with 24 academic researchers. Analysis of the researchers' description of their learning and thinking processes shows that the effects of IT on higher order thinking strategies can be classified, following Perkins (1985), into first order effects and second order effects. First order effects of IT amplify or improve existing thinking strategies, without changing their nature, while second order effects of IT cause significant changes in the researchers' thinking strategies. The results demonstrate that both types of effects take place in authentic research settings, often existing side by side. This article explores several examples of the ways in which IT affects higher order thinking strategies (such as forming research questions, constructing models and evaluating information), examines the types of effects created by IT, the conditions required for these effects to take place, and the role of distributed cognition.

(Barzilai and Zohar 2006: 130)

KEY FEATURES OF ARTICLES

Having identified the main features of this sample abstract, Figure 7.1 (opposite) identifies six features in the article as a whole:

As Figure 7.1 shows, it is possible to conceptualise the shape of a journal article in terms of two inverse triangles. The contents move from the general to the specific and back to the general as the authors introduce their topic and progress via the abstract, introduction and method to the presentation and discussion of the results, and finally the concluding material.

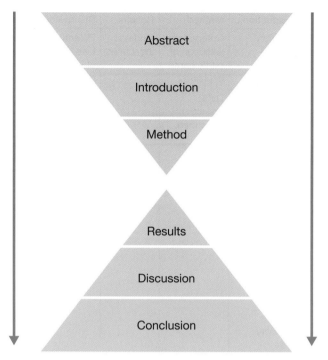

Figure 7.1 **The main features of a sample article on educational research**

Table 7.1 (overleaf) provides more information about the characteristics of each of the features in this sample article.

ANALYSIS OF A SAMPLE ARTICLE

Introduction

The topic of this sample article is clearly stated at the start of the introduction:

> **Introduction**
>
> This study revisits a classic yet still intriguing question regarding information technology (IT): what difference does IT 'really' make, in terms of people's thinking? Can IT cause significant modifications in the ways in which people act and think, or does it merely amplify and/or facilitate human activity without really changing it?
>
> (Barzilai and Zohar 2006: 130)

The authors gain the attention of their readers by introducing their research question about the effects of information technology on people's thinking as an 'intriguing' issue (Barzilai and Zohar 2006: 130). In your own academic writing, you can attract

Abstract	Introduction	Method	Results	Discussion	Conclusion
Research question identified	Research question reiterated	Criteria for selection of participants explained	Findings indentified	Potential bias of study discussed	Research question addressed again
Scope and contribution of study set out	Scope and contribution of study set out in more detail	Data collection described.		Other factors/ influences identified which may affect/ distort data collection and analysis	Significance of findings summarised
	Literature review	Limitations identified			Further research identified
	Key terms defined				
	Rationale given for study				
	Purpose of study explained				
	Claim to originality made				

Table 7.1 **The characteristics of features in a sample article**

your readers' attention in a similar way by thinking critically about your subject and identifying why it is important to explore.

Literature review

In this article, under the sub-heading 'Theoretical background', the authors map the literature in their field in three sections, and as they do this they define the key terms of 'first order' and 'second order' thinking strategies, based on Perkins (1985). They broadly describe first order as changes in the quantity of research it is possible to conduct online, whilst second order effects represent differences in the quality of research conducted online. This prepares the way for their argument that information technology affects both types of thinking as part of academic research.

As the authors acknowledge, a potential critique of this approach could be that these terms are constructs, and it is problematic to distinguish between higher and lower orders of intellectual activity (Haggis 2003). Their observation that 'in reality the border between quantity and quality is somewhat fuzzy' demonstrates their own critical thinking on the topic (2006: 132). Another possible critique is that since 2006 when Barzilai and Zohar's article was published, the use of information technology for research and education has developed considerably. Remember that when you are reading scholarly articles it is essential to reflect critically on the contents to identify both the strengths and the weaknesses of a source for your own research.

The authors identify gaps in the existing literature, for instance, they point out that the effects of print technology on people's thinking have been explored (Perkins 1985, Barzilai and Zohar 2006: 131) and they draw on this research to analyse the effects of information technology on academic work. They state their main contribution under the heading, 'Rationale and purpose of the study' as indicated below.

Rationale and purpose of the study

Unlike studies that focus on the effects computers may have on the learning processes of school students at various levels, this study examines the influence of IT on academic researchers whom we consider experts who are already experienced thinkers. The aim of examining experts is to learn how computers affect the thinking processes of people who are skilled and effective researchers. The ways in which these researchers think with computers may demonstrate desired outcomes of learning with computers, and thus contribute to the design of a model of teaching and learning for schools in computerized environments.

(Barzilai and Zohar 2006: 133)

Method

In the method section, the authors explain their process of data collection and provide evidence that they have thought critically about their procedures. For instance, they have gathered both qualitative data through semi-structured interviews and quantitative data through a survey on participants' use of computer applications for academic research. These two types of data were inter-validated as they analysed their findings, demonstrating one of the authors efforts to reduce the bias of their research.

Data collection method

- Participants (24 academics interviewed about their use of computers to conduct research)
- Academic experience (choice of academics justified and fact that they all started researching before computers become commonly used explained)
- Level of computer use (all participants use computers regularly for research)

- Academic disciplines (a scientific discipline, Life Sciences and a humanities subject, Judaic studies)
- Willingness to participate in the study (participants were self-selecting)
- Instrumentation (semi-structured interviews lasting a maximum of 90 minutes and a survey of computer use)
- Data collection and analysis (based on Grounded Theory)
- Limitations (potential gaps or areas of bias).

(Barzilai and Zohar 2006)

Limitations

All writing contains subjective elements and all research has limitations but in academic texts, both writers and readers are expected to demonstrate awareness of these unavoidable factors and their implications. Barzilai and Zohar demonstrate best practice as researchers by identifying the limitations of their study, which include the following:

Limitations identified by the authors

- Small sample size (24 participants)
- Participants taken from just two disciplines (Life Sciences and Judaic studies)
- The 'retrospective' nature of the interview (potentially not a realistic record as changes happened over a long period)
- Other factors probably influenced the academics' thinking processes, such as 'their growing knowledge and experience'
- The participants perceptions of computer use may be affected by factors beyond the scope of the study such as motivation, thinking styles, and positive attitudes towards innovation via IT.

(Barzilai and Zohar 2006: 135–42)

When you are thinking critically about the journal articles you have chosen to read for your own projects, it is essential to reflect on the limitations. With practice this will become easier because you will notice similar limitations in different articles. Often the authors of articles demonstrate their own rigour as do Barzilai and Zohar by identifying the limitations, but if you can perceive potential additional limitations you will demonstrate your strength as a critical thinker.

Potential additional limitations

- The key terms of first and second order thinking are arguably problematic constructs (Haggis 2003)
- Data could have been collected from more than one institution or national context
- Participants were self-selecting, which may mean they were biased in favour of using computers for research
- Data were collected from academics who use IT to conduct research, yet the findings are applied to using IT to each in schools
- Arguably, few negative impacts of computers are identified or fully discussed
- Arguably, generalisations are made about the applicability of the findings whereas they actually provide insights into the behaviour and perceptions of 24 academics
- Published in 2006, there may have been significant changes to use of IT which may impact on the findings.

Results

The study yielded a range of results which are clearly set out in the article.

Several effects of IT which Barzilai and Zohar identifiy through their data collection are treated in more detail, including forming research questions, creating new connections, building models, and evaluating information when working online.

Results

- All participants perceived computers as having effects on their thinking processes
- These are categorised as first and second order effects
- A substantial minority of participants (20.9%) perceive only first order effects (e.g. greater efficiency as a researcher)
- A majority of participants (66.6%) perceive first and second order effects
- A minority of participants (12.5%) perceive only second order effects (fundamental and long-term impacts on their thinking for research).

(Barzilai and Zohar 2006)

Discussion

Overall, this article presents computers as having beneficial impacts on academics' thinking strategies, and the authors address this finding in the discussion section of their article.

> ### Discussion
>
> The purpose of this study was to characterize the effects of IT on higher order thinking strategies in authentic research settings. Our findings show that two types of effects occur frequently: first order effects in which existing thinking strategies are amplified but remain unchanged, and second order effects in which thinking strategies are altered and new strategies are formed. This indicates that IT is indeed fundamentally reshaping scientific thinking.
>
> (Barzilai and Zohar 2006: 141)

The two main negative impacts of using computers to conduct academic research identified by Barzilai and Zohar are potententially less engagement with research, and an information overload. These are described by the participants as 'a risk of becoming superficial' when computers process information, and being swamped by a 'sea of information'. As mentioned above, use of information technology has increased since 2006, and as a consequence these negative impacts of using computers may be perceived differently today.

Conclusion

The article closes with suggestions for further research in the conclusion section:

> ### Conclusion
>
> The fact that IT indeed creates second order changes in higher order thinking strategies suggests, in our opinion, that these strategies do have a distributed nature, and that they reflect a growing 'intellectual partnership' between people and computers. To conclude, our findings show that a study of how experts work and think with computers may offer us valuable insights regarding future possible developments of peoples' thinking in a technological society.
>
> (Barzilai and Zohar 2006: 143)

At the end of their article, Barzilai and Zohar answer their research question, writing that 'IT is indeed fundamentally reshaping scientific thinking' (2006: 141). By attending to their research question throughout the article and addressing it clearly at the end, Barzilai and Zohar demonstrate best practice as critical thinkers. In your own research writing, try to do the same by focusing on your main point, addressing it from a range of angles, and in the light of different existing research.

To sum up

This analysis of a sample journal article shows how the authors articulate their research question, then take their readers from a general discussion of the topic through the introduction and method sections to the crux of their study where they present their results. Having presented their findings, the authors gradually extend the scope of their focus through the discussion section, and reflect on the wider implications as they close the article.

The conclusion of a scholarly article is an excellent section to analyse because you can often spot implications or applications for your own area of interest. As you read the conclusion, ask yourself whether there are any weaknesses or gaps you could identify, but also consider the strength of the source.

In this article, the authors turn as they close to the subject of 'setting educational goals and planning how to integrate IT in school' (Barzilai and Zohar 2006: 143). However, it would also be possible to build on the finding that computers can affect people's thinking strategies in other ways, for instance by conducting further studies of how undergraduate dissertation writers are aided or hindered in completing their projects by information technology. As you read articles try to think of alternative applications for the ideas they contain.

SUMMARY

This chapter has analysed a sample journal article in the field of educational research to help you become more familiar with some of the conventions of research writing. Although the articles in your own subject area will differ from this example, the tips in this chapter will give you a headstart as you think critically about the sources you read so you can draw on them as possible models for your own research writing.

The main arguments in this chapter were:

- Abstracts give you important clues about the relevance of journal articles for your own writing
- It is important to familiarise yourself with the conventions of research writing in your field
- As you prepare to write, you should identify the limitations in the sources you read and critique them as appropriate.

References

Barzilai, S. and Zohar, A. (2006) How Does Information Technology Shape Thinking? *Thinking Skills and Creativity* 1: 130–145.

Haggis, T. (2003) Constructing Images of Ourselves? A Critical Investigation into 'Approaches to Learning Research in Higher Education'. *British Educational Research Journal* 29 (1): 89–104.

Perkins, D. N. (1985) The Fingertip Effect: How Information Processing Technology Changes Thinking. *Educational Researcher* 14 (7):11–17.

PART 4

REFLECTION

Reflective practice is fundamental to effective critical thinking, and it enables you to identify your own strengths and weaknesses, and thus learn from your experiences. Reflective practice is often determined by the conventions in your discipline and is influenced by your preferred learning style, so it is important that you adapt the tips in this section to your own personality and disciplinary context.

- Reflect on your personal, academic and professional experiences
- Identify your strengths and weaknesses
- Identify your own aims
- Set yourself concrete objectives to achieve these aims.

8 ▶ REFLECTIVE CRITICAL THINKING

This chapter investigates the role of reflective thinking as well as making decisions and clarifying your own ideas. It offers advice about asking yourself useful questions, being open-minded, and sticking to the point. You should use the suggestions in this chapter as a starting point and try to develop your own strategies for becoming a more reflectve and effective thinker.

This chapter covers:

- Four steps to help your thinking
    1 Look at your questions
    2 Do not be closed-minded
    3 Clarify your thinking
    4 Stick to the point.

Using this chapter

Topic	Page
Four steps to help your thinking	88
1 Look at your questions	89
2 Do not be closed-minded	89
3 Clarify your thinking	90
4 Stick to the point	93

INTRODUCTION

Critical thinking is characterised not simply by the ability to critique other people's work, but also to think through and reconsider our own ideas. In many ways, reconsidering our own ideas is a more difficult task than identifying the weaknesses in other people's ideas. We all carry on inner dialogues – discussions played out in our heads – in which we think of what we should have said, or why the other person was wrong. We do not realise as often that we may have been wrong or made a mistake. However, thinking critically requires us to look as closely at our own thoughts and ideas as we examine other people's.

This is quite different, incidentally, from worrying or being insecure about your performance. Some people lack self-confidence and the ability to appreciate when their performance is going well. Critical reflection should build confidence; after a fair evaluation, your ideas will be clearer and more firmly based on good evidence. Critical thinking should be balanced, and unfair or unreasonable self-criticism is as destructive as tearing down other people unfairly.

Have you ever thought about how you think? When was the last time you recognised that you had not considered an important aspect of a problem? Have you tried to make sure that you have systematically considered every side of an issue? How did you go about that? What would be involved in a systematic consideration of something?

Critical thinking involves inspecting our own thinking processes. How do we generate new ideas? Are there times or activities that help each of us to come up with new ideas? (For example, when do you have your best ideas? Do you think better in the morning or in the evening?) Are there values that you have that you would not violate, or that shape the way you behave? These are questions that cannot be answered for you, but many people cannot answer them for themselves. To be a critical thinker, you need to inspect your own thought processes.

FOUR STEPS TO HELP YOUR THINKING

The following steps are essentially practical ways of looking at the day-to-day questions which confront us that we must solve to get on in university or in our daily business. Critical thinking involves solving problems like these, but it also requires deeper thinking.

1 Look at your questions
2 Do not be closed-minded
3 Clarify your thinking
4 Stick to the point.

These four steps will help you think more clearly, but they are not in themselves simple or easy to do.

1 Look at your questions

The first step is to be clear in your thinking: what is the idea, issue or problem that you are considering? If it is an opinion, what exactly is your opinion? State the idea, problem, issue or opinion as clearly as you can. Writing the problem down will probably help. When you express your ideas on paper it is easier to think about other ways of formulating the problem. Goody (1977) argues that literacy – learning to read and write – fundamentally changed the way that we think, so ideas that were vague and imprecise when people could only talk became fixed and clearer when people began to read and to write. Many people have questioned whether the development of writing and reading skills had such a far-reaching effect, but most of us recognise that writing down an idea forces us to be clearer.

In addition, discuss the problem with another person. One of the most important components of good critical thinking is getting out of our own limited viewpoints. Another person will bring a different perspective, and that perspective will help you to reconsider your ideas.

2 Do not be closed-minded

Generating ideas

- ■ Set a fixed time and stick to it
- ■ Write down as many different ideas as possible
- ■ Do not judge the ideas!
- ■ Can the ideas you have come up with be combined to make a better idea?

When you are thinking through a problem or idea, try not to be closed-minded. Instead, be open to as many possibilities as you can. One way to generate more ideas is to set yourself (or, with friends if possible) a specific period of time in which you will think of possible solutions to the problem or alternative approaches to the idea. This should be relatively short – if you are alone, perhaps no more than 10 or 15 minutes. Think of as many different ideas as possible and jot them down.

Do not judge these ideas! Simply write them down, and focus on generating different ideas.

At the end of the set time, look at the ideas you have written down. Can some of the ideas be joined together to make a better, more developed idea?

Other approaches include sleeping on a problem. Many people find that new ideas occur to them when they are not specifically focused on the problem, so going to bed after a period of working on a problem may generate new ideas or approaches. Be sure that you have a notepad by your bed because you may not remember your good ideas in the morning! Besides sleeping on a problem, there are other types of distraction or ways of distancing yourself and letting your mind roam freely. Exercise, hoovering, or washing-up work for some people. In general, though, you have to engage in the activity in ways that let your mind move freely, which may mean you have to put away the devices that can engage our minds during boring tasks, such as listening to music or watching television. Finding new ideas this way requires good time management, since ideas don't always arise on demand.

A final idea that you can consider for generating new approaches is to look for ideas that contradict the ideas you already have. Scholars who do qualitative research look for 'discomfiting data', that is, facts which contradict the ideas they are currently considering. This is a strong, knowledge-based approach to reflection, and one that we don't use often enough. It requires us to take the ideas or arguments of people we disagree with seriously and consider them as possibilities.

In all of these cases, the essential element is to take a non-judgemental approach to the ideas that you are generating.

3 Clarify your thinking

There are three questions you can ask which will help you clarify your thinking:

- **Can I express my idea in a different way?**
- **Can I elaborate on the point I want to make?**
- **Can I give an illustration or example?**

To take a simple example, consider whether or not to replace your computer. (If you have one; if not, consider whether to get one, or consider another costly purchase you might make, one that you'd have to think over.)

An example of decision-making

Write down a simple statement of the issue:

I should get new computer.

Now, around that statement, or in lists underneath, write some of the reasons for and against the issue. This process is illustrated in Figure 8.1 opposite.

Your list could also look something like Figure 8.2, but with different reasons for and against.

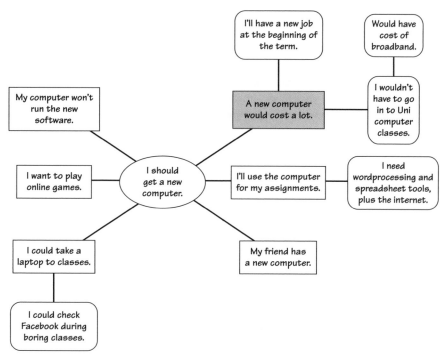

Figure 8.1 **Generating ideas**

FOR		AGAINST	
Things I could do	Other reasons		Offsets
Takes notes in class Work on assignments Use new video editing software	Would be better than my friend's computer	Cost!	Could pay for it with part-time salary Wouldn't need to pay for travel to Uni so often – could work at home
		Would need to get broadband	Could share costs with housemates

Figure 8.2 **Generating ideas for and against**

However, can the reasons for or against be grouped or clustered? For example, study needs, such as working on assignments or note-taking in lectures, can be grouped together. On the other hand, fun uses, such as going on Facebook or playing online games, might be another category. Both of these could be grouped together as possibilities that a new computer would enable. In a different category would be keeping up with a friend who has a new computer. These categories might be called 'What you can do' and 'What you get from owning.' In the negative category is the cost. This might be offset by income from a new job or the savings from not having to go in to the university to work on assignments.

Out of these two lists of ideas for and against, you would then have to decide which are your real or most important motives. In the column listing reasons for getting a computer, would you rather do something, or own something? Do you want the computer in order to work better at university, or in order to play more? In the other column, against, there are costs. These might be met by savings on travel expenses or more efficient use of your time, although whether this would be enough to justify the purchase would also be an important part of your thinking.

To recognise that you want a computer in order to play games or go on social networking sites is not to say that you should not get a computer. It might affect the type of computer you plan to buy. A computer for games might need to be more powerful and more expensive, while a computer for online activities like social networking might need less speed and be less expensive. Even if you decided that you wanted the computer in order to have one that is as new, attractive or powerful as your friend's computer, that would identify what you wanted the computer for, and set a mark for the qualities which are most important for you.

Clear critical thinking does not automatically provide the right answer, but it does help you look for answers in the right places. If you understand what it is that you want, then you can make a decision for the right reasons. If you are unclear in your thinking, you might justify buying a computer to help you study, and be disappointed because it is not powerful enough for games or attractive enough to compare with your friend's computer. Reflective critical thinking requires honesty with yourself and a willingness to be patient. It will not point you towards the quickest or easiest decision.

The economist John Kay (2010) has pointed out that lists like this have been used for over 200 years. Their prime difficulty is that as well as being used to balance issues in order to achieve an informed decision, they can be manipulated to achieve an outcome that was determined before the issues were balanced. Charles Darwin tried to balance the choice between marrying and staying unmarried by the use of a table similar to the decision table for deciding whether to buy a computer.

According to Kay (2010), Darwin understood the impossibility of making such a decision through the use of a decision table and, within a year of writing the table, he married the woman who was to be with him for the rest of his life. In fact, decision tables may be used to find 'a weighty and carefully analysed rationale for a decision that has already been made' (Kay 2010: 90). We create a decision table to justify what we want to do, and to permit ourselves to do what we have already decided to do.

This is one reason why critical thinking must be grounded in reflection and self-awareness. If you use a decision table to justify the inclination that you brought to the question, you need to think more deeply about the question you are analysing. The decision that you want to take might be the correct one, but you must not pretend that you have considered it more deeply if your table only justifies your original inclination.

4 Stick to the point

When you are considering an idea critically, it is important to stick to that idea and not to be distracted by other thoughts. Clear, critical thinking is hard work. One thought may lead to another that seems related but, before you notice, you have drifted away from the question you need to answer. Ask yourself, is this relevant? Does it contribute to answering the question I am asking? If not, get back to the point!

Of course, it may be that you can't stick to the point because you disagree with or oppose the idea, but you don't recognise your own opposition. This can happen when, for example, we have values that we are not aware of. To return to the simple example of buying a computer, you may be financially cautious or you may not value the showiness of a new computer. Even though the table in Figure 8.2 suggests you should buy a computer, you don't agree. As in the example of Darwin and his consideration of whether to marry or not, he realised that whatever the table he had made suggested, this was not how to make a decision of this sort.

This, too, is reflectiveness in practice. Critical reflection requires you to inspect your thought processes at every step. Sometimes, the failure of our thought processes (as in the inability to stick to the point) illuminates our true desires.

SUMMARY

This chapter has emphasised that critical thinking requires reflection about your own thinking processes. It has suggested some steps which may help you think more clearly and consider your ideas in a critical light.

The main arguments in this chapter were:

- Look at the questions you are asking. Are they clear?
- Do not be closed-minded. Consider as many possibilities as you can
- Clarify your thinking
- Stick to the point.

References

Goody, J. (1977) *The Domestication of the Savage Mind*. Cambridge: Cambridge University Press.

Kay, J. (2010) *Oblinquity*. London: Profile Books.

9 ▶ YOUR CAREER

This chapter points out that the critical thinking skills you develop in academia are transferable to your future professional context. It continues to focus on reflectivity and independent thinking in order to support your development of the specific knowledge and skills necessary to succeed in your chosen career.

This chapter covers:

- Transferable critical thinking skills
- Criticality and your career
- Your career ambitions.

Using this chapter

Topic	Page
Transferable critical thinking skills	96
Reflectivity	97
Independence	97
Connections	97
Criticality and your career	98
The job description	98
Reading the job description critically	100
Reading the person specification critically	100
Relating the person specification to yourself	102
Your career ambitions	104
Skills	104
Knowledge	104
Experience	107

INTRODUCTION

This chapter helps you begin to draw upon critical thinking to plan for your own professional development. It argues that it is vital to start thinking about your career while you are still studying because this gives you the most time to develop in the areas required for the types of jobs that appeal to you.

TRANSFERABLE CRITICAL THINKING SKILLS

Whilst studying at an advanced level you are developing transferable critical thinking skills, and this is one of the reasons why employers often appreciate graduate applicants. University study fosters critical thinking by requiring you to undertake research projects which involve locating relevant information, processing vast quantities of data, and developing a critical perspective that enables you and others to make use of your discoveries. Figure 9.1 lists eight components of critical thinking and identifies some ways in which these capabilities apply to professional contexts.

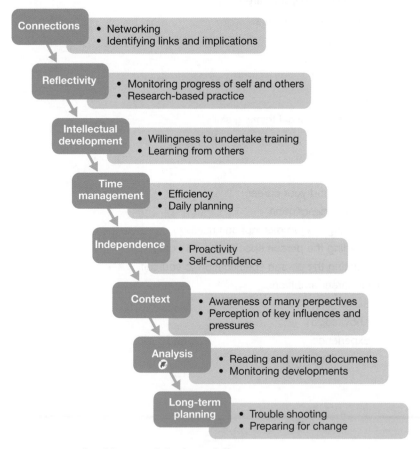

Figure 9.1 **Transferable critical thinking skills**

Reflectivity

This capability is especially relevant to the workplace; for instance, a person who is not reflective is unlikely to be very self-aware and may not be ready to admit to making poor professional judgements. Although everyone makes occasional errors, employers value openness and, if they identify a lack of reflectivity in a candidate who is applying for a position, this might be a reason to select an alternative applicant.

Independence

Similarly, a person who does not show independence when applying for a job is unlikely to be good at negotiating with others or being assertive at appropriate times. These competencies are essential within business to clinch deals, and are vital in many other professions because they enable individuals to cultivate respect in the workplace. Demonstrating independence as you apply for a position may give you an extra boost as a prospective employee, whereas failure to display this quality could work against you as an applicant.

Connections

In addition, a person who is not able to make connections with colleagues is unlikely to liaise productively and network within and beyond a professional organisation. In most contexts, including industrial, commercial, government, and academic careers, employees are expected to initiate and sustain strong working relationships, and if your potential employer perceives a lack of interpersonal skills when interviewing you, this could also be a reason for offering the job to another candidate.

The ability to make connections is not just about working with others, in terms of critical thinking it also means perceiving links between ideas and piecing together disparate kinds of data to gain insights into complex problems or topics. This ability is of paramount importance in a range of career contexts, and demonstrating competence in this area will help to give you the edge over your competitors. Whilst studying for your degree you are developing your capacity to make connections between ideas by learning about the theoretical perspectives associated with your academic field.

As you apply for jobs, you can use examples from your academic experience to evidence your aptitude for professional spheres, and now is the time to start considering how you can transfer the critical thinking skills you are developing at university into the context of your chosen career path. However, if you are not yet sure about which profession you wish to enter, critical thinking becomes even more important because drawing on your ability to reflect, make connections and undertake long-term planning, you can work towards forming a clearer idea of the professional sphere in which you are most likely to thrive. Throughout your career, you will transfer the strategies you develop at university into new and dynamic contexts, but first you should consider how to exploit the skills you have already begun to display.

CRITICALITY AND YOUR CAREER

When you start to look at job applications in earnest, you will see that there are two main types of criteria that prospective employers use to select the strongest candidates.

Two types of selection criteria

■ The job description

■ The person specification.

The job description

Figure 9.2 is an example of a job description adapted from a post advertised in the field of adult social care based at Leeds City Council in the UK. As you read this job description, consider how critical thinking skills relate to the main duties described. Do not be put off by the detail in this job description. This is common, and the sooner you practise analysing this kind of information, the better prepared you will be when you begin applying for positions of your own.

LEEDS CITY COUNCIL JOB DESCRIPTION	
DEPARTMENT: Adult Social Care	
SECTION / ESTABLISHMENT: Commissioning Services	
POST TITLE: ASSISTANT COMMISSIONING OFFICER and PERFORMANCE ASSURANCE	GRADE: SO 2
POST(S) TO WHICH DIRECTLY RESPONSIBLE: ADULT COMMISSIONING MANAGER	
POSTS(S) FOR WHICH DIRECTLY RESPONSIBLE: ADMINISTRATORS / ADMINISTRATIVE ASSISTANTS	
PURPOSE OF THE JOB: To support and facilitate the work of the Commissioning Services directorate by supporting Managers and Officers engaged in the administration of Contracts, Grant funding, Performance and Quality assurance of social care activity. Ensuring the establishment, maintenance and review of effective monitoring and information systems. Taking responsibility for the administration of stakeholder surveys and the timely production of reports related to this. **RESPONSIBILITIES:** • To assist the Commissioning Officers in the work with providers and suppliers, and potential providers, to build effective working relationships to ensure long term and sustainable social care services are available, including both statutory and universal. Identifying and developing the capacity of providers across all market sectors	

Figure 9.2 A sample job description in the field of social care (Leeds City Council 2010)

- Where appropriate, participate in market testing exercises and management through the letting of contracts, analysis, research and budget monitoring
- To participate in Employee Development Schemes/Appraisal/Supervision and contribute to the identification of your own development needs in line with business requirements
- To assist officers in developing efficient processes for the efficient running of the section and/or wider contracting or performance issues.
- To assist commissioning officers in drafting contract or tender documents
- To assist officers in work in conjunction with the relevant Finance Officers to monitor expenditure and ensure financial targets are met
- Where appropriate, to assist officers in conjunction with Contract holders in monitoring and evaluating contract performance; ensuring contract terms and conditions are fulfilled and enforced, if necessary. Demonstrating that external contracts and SLAs deliver value for money and high quality services
- To maintain accurate records of spending related to grants, providing regular reports as required
- Where appropriate, to organise and administer procedures for payments to service users and carers and voluntary sector representatives, keeping records of the expenditure
- To maintain and update information about contracts, providers and/or contractors in an accessible format
- Maintenance of effective performance assurance systems
- To maintain and update service utilisation information in an accessible format
- To disseminate accessible and regular information to all stakeholders in a systematised way (including any website facility or development)
- To monitor the effectiveness of provision of services by the collection, storage and analysis of data supplied by external and internal providers
- To provide a point of contact for internal and external service providers for enquiries and information about the investment and grants programmes, and – where appropriate – co-ordinate the dissemination of information on and applications for such programmes
- To ensure the provision of practical administrative support to Officers with responsibility for grant allocation and the contracts associated with such grant funding and/or the maintenance of effective performance assurance systems
- Where appropriate, to service the investment and grants panels which report to the project board: act as the point of contact
- To maintain and update relevant databases: gather baseline information including stakeholder surveys, keep monitoring information on all aspects of contracts/grant and/or quality assurance programmes, providing updates as required for any appropriate project board/officer of elected member forum
- Where appropriate, to supervise the work of administrative assistants as required for the successful delivery of projects supported by this post
- To participate in and provide training and development activities as necessary to ensure up-to-date knowledge, skills and continuous professional development
- To participate in and provide training and development activities as necessary to ensure up-to-date knowledge and skills
- To undertake other duties appropriate to the post as required by the Commissioning Manager
- To comply with the requirements of all Leeds City Council and Departmental policies, procedures and staff instructions, including responsibilities under the Health and Safety Policy and Procedures
- To actively promote and support Leeds City Council's and Departmental Policies on Equal Opportunities and to work in an anti-oppressive manner

Figure 9.2 continued

Reading the job description critically

You can think critically about this job description as a text, which will give you the best insight into how to respond when you are applying for jobs in your own area of interest. This involves careful reading to absorb and understand the information in order to interpret it in terms of the implications for you as a potential job applicant. In particular, you can consider how the requirements listed in Figure 9.2 relate to your own experiences and strengths.

As this is just an example of a job description, you should apply your close reading skills when you are applying for positions in your own field of expertise. For example, you could exploit your knowledge of the eight components of critical thinking discussed previously to analyse the range of duties listed in a job description that interests you. These eight components are outlined again below.

> ## Criticality and your career
> 1 **Connections**
> 2 **Reflectivity**
> 3 **Independence**
> 4 **Time management**
> 5 **Intellectual development**
> 6 **Context**
> 7 **Analysis**
> 8 **Long-term planning.**

In Table 9.1 (opposite) the main responsibilities of this position are broadly categorised according to these eight components of critical thinking.

The key components of critical thinking are essential in every career. In addition to demonstrating your critical thinking skills as a prospective candidate, you need to draw on your ability to analyse information as you prepare to present yourself during the application process.

Reading the person specification critically

Whichever type of career you are interested in, you should prepare to succeed in that specialism by getting to know your natural abilities and working to strengthen your capabilities in other areas. You can do this either by gaining diverse experience to practise the abilities you find most difficult, or by seeking opportunities to undertake specific training, for instance in time management techniques.

Figure 9.3 (p. 103) is an example of a person specification adapted from the aforementioned post in adult social care at Leeds City Council in the UK. As you read this

Connections	Reflectivity	Independence	Time management	Intellectual development	Context	Analysis	Long-term planning
Build effective working relationships	Ensure value for money and high quality	Draft documents	Develop efficient processes	Identify own development needs	Disseminate information to stakeholders in a systematised way (including online)	Undertake contracts analysis, research and budget monitoring	Monitor and evaluate provision/performance
Act as point of contact	Maintain effective performance assurance systems	Organise procedures for payments	Maintain records and produce regular reports	Participate in and provide training/professional development	Coordinate dissemination of information	Monitor expenditure and ensure targets are met	Comply with policies and procedures
		Supervise the work of others				Monitor, maintain and update information/databases	Promote equal opportunities

Table 9.1 The main responsibilities of the post organised into components of critical thinking

person specification, consider how critical thinking relates to the skills, experience and knowledge required by the successful applicant for this post.

Notice the three columns on the right hand side. 'Ess' stands for 'Essential' requirements for this post, and any applicant who does not demonstrate these abilities will not be short-listed for an interview. So, when you are applying for jobs in the future, ensure that you align your application with the qualities identified as essential.

'Des' stands for 'Desirable' and applicants who display experience and ability in these areas will have a strong advantage over those who do not. 'MOA' stands for 'Method of Assessment'. For graduate-level jobs, five methods of assessing candidates' suitability are:

- The application form
- The *curriculum vitae*
- The job interview
- A presentation, test or activity set as part of the selection process
- Certificates of qualifications.

In Figure 9.3 opposite, the Methods of Assessment for each criterion are coded in the following way:

A = Application form
I = Interview

So, looking at the first line of the person specification, a candidate's ability to plan workload and time effectively will be assessed by the application form and the interview (A/I). That means that you would need to mention in your application how you have planned your workload and time in the past at work or university. You should also be prepared to answer questions about this if you are invited to an interview.

Relating the person specification to yourself

Presenting yourself as the best candidate is far easier if you have thought about the qualities you have to offer and can match these to the stated requirements of a professional role. Remember to think laterally if you do not have experience of the specific areas listed in a person specification or job description. Often it is possible to translate the experience you do possess into more relevant terms, so look at the language used by prospective employers and try to re-phrase these terms as the skills you know you possess.

For example, you may not have direct experience of 'monitoring performance' in the workplace, but in most academic disciplines you are trained to monitor data or events and apply the insights to make recommendations. For instance, if your academic discipline is science you might have conducted experiments, observed the outcomes and written reports. Or, if your field is health you might have

LEEDS CITY COUNCIL PERSON SPECIFICATION			
SKILLS	**Ess**	**Des**	**MOA**
• Able to plan your own workload and time effectively	*		A/I
• Investigative, analytical and interpretive skills	*		A/I
• Able to use and maintain databases	*		A/I
• Able to monitor and analyse budgetary information	*		A/I
• Administrative and organisational skills	*		A/I
• Able to provide clear information to all stakeholders, including staff and service users and carers	*		A/I
• Able to work well with people of all backgrounds and from different organisations	*		A/I
• Able to supervise the work of administrative assistants	*		A/I
• High level of computer literacy and willing to develop new skills in IT	*		A/I
• Able to support staff in planning and developing services	*		A/I
• Capacity for creative thought	*		A/I
• Flexible and adaptable	*		A/I
• Ability to work with a wide range of stakeholders internal and external to the Council		*	A/I
KNOWLEDGE/QUALIFICATIONS	**Ess**	**Des**	**MOA**
• Understanding of monitoring performance/projects and/or budgets	*		A/I
• Understanding of contracting practice	*		A/I
• Understanding of health and social care issues, particularly in terms of the role of the voluntary and community sector and partnership work		*	A/I
• Knowledge of the voluntary and community sector		*	A/I
• Understanding of the role of IT systems within health and social care services		*	A/I
EXPERIENCE	**Ess**	**Des**	**MOA**
• Of using and maintaining databases	*		A/I
• Of producing information and reports using IT	*		A/I
• Of organising meetings and events	*		A/I
• Of producing publicity information	*		A/I
• Of contributing to planning or commissioning work within a health or social care environment		*	A/I
• Of working with members and officers within a local authority or health setting		*	A/I
• Of budget control, preferably within a health or social care setting		*	A/I
• Of working with service users and carers within the context of health and social care		*	A/I
• Some experience of website design			

Figure 9.3 **A sample person specification in the field of social care**
(Leeds City Council 2010)

undertaken observations to report on the implications. Similarly, if your subject is business you may have followed current affairs or undertaken research in order to produce a report.

YOUR CAREER AMBITIONS

Although the skills, knowledge and experience outlined above are specific requirements of this position, these qualities are also components of critical thinking. Considering them in this way reveals that many of these attributes are common requirements of employers in other fields, including industry, academic and commerce.

Skills

In Table 9.2 opposite, the skills outlined in the sample person specification are listed under one of the eight components of critical thinking previously discussed. Clearly, there are other aspects of criticality, and the items in the job specification could have been differently arranged, but the main purpose of this table is to demonstrate how you can begin to process and interpret information to better understand and exploit your own career opportunities.

In terms of the skills required for this post, you should be able to make connections with a variety of people by networking and liaising both internally and externally. Critical thinking should enable you to see things from another person's point of view, which will facilitate networking and getting on with other people. You should be reflective and able to demonstrate creativity at work, as well as being flexible in the face of change. The workplace changes rapidly, and only a person with good thinking skills will be able to anticipate change and react appropriately. You should be independent enough to supervise others and support them. Critical thinking will enable you to manage your time, plan your workload, and engage in long-term planning.

Whilst this job description is specific to a post in social care, you will be expected to demonstrate this range of critical thinking competencies regardless of your professional field. In your own career context there may be particular emphasis on one of these areas, such as the ability to work independently, or a facility to make connections and collaborate with others.

When you analyse the requirements of a particular post, work out which skills are prioritised by your prospective employer, and stress your ability in these as you apply and present yourself during job interviews.

Knowledge

In the above example, there is an even spread of requirements under most of the critical thinking components, but being aware of the context is not part of the skill-set for this position. In contrast, candidates are expected to display a strong awareness of the context when it comes to the 'knowledge' part of the person specification. In Table 9.3, the specific kinds of knowledge necessary for this post in social care are categorised under the same eight components of critical thinking.

Connections	Reflectivity	Independence	Time management	Intellectual development	Context	Analysis	Long-term planning
Provide clear information to stakeholders	Capacity for creative thought	Use and maintain databases	Plan own workload and time effectively	High level of computer literacy and willing to develop new IT skills		Investigative, analytical, and interpretive skills	Support others in planning and development
Work well with people from all backgrounds and organisations	Flexible and adaptable	Supervise the work of others	Administrative and organisational skills			Monitor and analyse budgetary information	

Table 9.2 The main skills required for this post organised into components of critical thinking

Connections	Reflectivity	Independence	Time management	Intellectual development	Context	Analysis	Long-term planning
Understanding of contracting practice		Using and maintaining databases	Organising meetings and events	Budget control	Understanding of health and social care issues	Monitoring performance, projects and budgets	Plan and commissioning work
Working with service users		Producing information, reports and publicity info.		Website design	Knowledge of the voluntary and community sector		
					Understanding of IT within health and social care		

Table 9.3 The main knowledge required for this post organised into components of critical thinking

In terms of the knowledge required for this post, candidates should be able to make connections between current best practice and the responsibilities of this role. If you don't know what current best practice is in the area that you are applying for a post in, you will need to research the area and find this out.

Although being reflective is not specified in the knowledge section, candidates will need to be reflective and be able to demonstrate creativity at work. Candidates will also need to be flexible in the face of change. Candidates should be independent enough to supervise others, as well as to support them and contribute to a smoothly functioning team. In addition, applicants should possess strong time management skills in order to plan personal workloads, and to plan for the future and that of the organisation. Candidates will need to be willing to develop within the role and to demonstrate potential for growth at the interview stage.

Experience

Most candidates coming from university draw on their educational background to demonstrate their experience, though many applicants will also have experience gathered from part-time (or full-time) employment and work in the voluntary sector. If you are unable to find paid work that is relevant to the area in which you wish to work, you should consider offering to help a charity or other voluntary organisation.

For example, in the case of the post that we are using as an example here, the person specification requires certain types of experience as essential for the post. These are shown in Table 9.4, which is adapted from the person specifications in Figure 9.3.

To show how volunteer experience might be used to demonstrate experience in these essential areas, suppose that you volunteered for a dogs rehoming centre. In this role, you might have worked in the offices as well as contributed to caring for the dogs. When you come to write your application, you could draw on this work to describe how you fulfilled these essential areas of experience. A dog rehoming centre would have to maintain a database of the dogs that were given to the centre, including facts about the dogs such as breed, weight and date of entry to the centre. You might have entered data, checked to see if there was an appropriate dog for someone who wanted to adopt or recorded the adoption of a dog. You might also have produced reports on the dogs, written up on the dog rehoming centre's

Experience	Essential	MOA
■ Of using and maintaining databases	*	A/I
■ Of producing information and reports using IT	*	A/I
■ Of organising meetings and events	*	A/I
■ Of producing publicity information	*	A/I

Table 9.4 Experience required for the post of Assistant Commissioning Officer
(adapted from Leeds City Council 2010)

computers. You could explain how you organised groups of people who wanted to adopt a pet and gave presentations to them. You might also be able to write about producing publicity for fund-raising events. These would all contribute to your application, and would demonstrate your experience in these essential areas.

Thinking critically and reflectively about your own work, volunteering, and educational experience will enable you to draw on this experience in applying for work after university. In fact, thinking critically while you are still studying would allow you to look for opportunities to gain experience, by asking managers or supervisors to let you take on responsibilities that would enhance your CV. Thinking this way is long-range planning, one of the key components of critical thinking.

SUMMARY

To summarise, your ability to become a strong critical thinker in your future professional context relates closely to the skills you are developing within academia. This chapter has suggested that the best way to give yourself an advantage when you leave university is to begin early in considering how you can best exploit your strengths as a critical thinker, so you can present yourself with confidence and clarity as you apply for jobs.

This chapter has demonstrated how to analyse job descriptions and break down the range of responsibilities into key components of critical thinking in order to see how you might transfer the skills you have developed into the career marketplace. In addition, this chapter has shown how to interpret person specifications by assessing how you can deliver in terms of the skills and knowledge required.

The main message of this chapter is that it is worth investing time and energy in developing competence as a critical thinker because this will enable you to achieve both your academic goals and your professional ambitions. Simply by being aware of the main components of critical thinking and assessing your strengths in these areas you will enhance your performance.

Prior to entering the world of work, knowing where your strengths lie and where you have potential weaknesses as a critical thinker can equip you to choose projects or courses that will offer opportunities to develop in new areas. The dissertation or final year project of an undergraduate degree is an excellent example of an academic activity through which you can develop professional competencies.

The main arguments in this chapter were:

- Get to know your own strengths and weaknesses
- Read critically when you are applying for a job
- Start to develop your critical thinking skills now!

References

Leeds City Council (2010) *Head of information management and technology*. http://jobs. leeds.gov.uk/JobDetails.aspx/5221/Assistant_Commissioning_Officer/?Ssimple=&SSectors=-1&SSalary=-1&STerm=19&Sdepartment_id=-1&SLocations=-1&SSchools=4&SSubjects=&o= [27 March 2010].

CONCLUSION

This book has focused on four aspects of critical thinking and analysis:

- **Reading**
- **Planning**
- **Writing**
- **Reflection.**

Each of these activities can be broken down into elements, although the tasks involved will differ depending on your learning style and the types of projects you undertake. To summarise, below are some of the points you may wish to consider as you undertake each of these aspects of critical thinking.

READING

Researching your topic thoroughly is an essential part of the critical thinking process, and the effort you put in at this early phase will pay dividends when you come to the writing stage. As critical thinking demands that you engage with sources and develop your own perspective on scholarly arguments, the more relevant texts you read, the better informed and more confident your own argument will be. However, it is dangerous to read without considering your own eventual argument because without knowing why you are reading, you are more likely to waste time on texts which turn out to be irrelevant for your purpose. Assess your own needs and the requirements of your project before collecting sources (Lunsford 2005: 139). You can do this by re-reading your aim or assignment brief, and jotting down the key words as prompts for your research.

Reading

- Check out the sources your tutors recommend
- Also undertake independent research
- Get advice from specialists in your university library
- Do not take sources at face value, but analyse the contents
- Make notes of the author, date, page numbers and publication details in order to cite and reference your sources fully.

PLANNING

Consider the eight components of critical thinking outlined in this book, but remain open-minded because this is not an exhaustive list of the issues you should bear in mind as you plan your academic assignments. Above all, work on improving your ability to assess the time you have available for each project, and use this valuable resource wisely (Wallas 1926).

Planning

- Work on your time management
- Think about the parameters of your research for each project
- Remember your word limit
- Be aware of your other commitments
- Give yourself sufficient thinking time to develop innovative approaches and ideas.

WRITING

Build upon the models of successful academic writing you find, for instance, in journals, but do not forget that you should approach all the examples of scholarly writing you find with an analytic eye. Avoid adopting any method of organising your ideas without reflecting on the strengths and weaknesses for your own purpose. Remember that although it is useful to read within your field, it can also be advantageous to read outside your subject area to gain different perspectives on the issues you are studying.

As a critical thinker you should try to adapt the models of effective writing you find and organise your ideas in innovative ways. Maintain some caution though, and if possible produce a plan and check this with your tutor before spending lots of time drafting an assignment. As you seek out positive examples of scholarly writing from a range of contexts, ask yourself whether you can play with the conventions you observe to develop your own approaches and generate new perspectives on the issues you are studying.

Writing

- Read widely to enhance your own academic writing
- Interrogate the models you find
- Credit the authors by referencing clearly
- Take time to discuss your ideas and plan your projects
- Revise your writing with care
- Edit your writing prior to submission.

REFLECTION

As you read about new ways of approaching the process of critical thinking, other possibilities for reflective practice will occur to you depending on your interests and experiences and, with commitment to enhancing your criticality, you can improve your own performance both in academia and beyond.

Reflection

- Reflect in order to learn from your experiences
- Get to know your own strengths and weaknesses
- Be prepared to doubt your own ideas
- Identify your aims in academia and beyond
- Set yourself concrete objectives to achieve your aims.

SUMMARY

The suggestions in this book are just starting points for you to consider how you can make your own contributions as a scholar and professional, and the topics which have been discussed are not the only areas deserving your attention, although they are crucial to developing your competence as a critical thinker. Critical thinking is a process but, as previously mentioned, this process is nonlinear, and the individual components can spark with each other in many different ways, as is reiterated in Figure C.1.

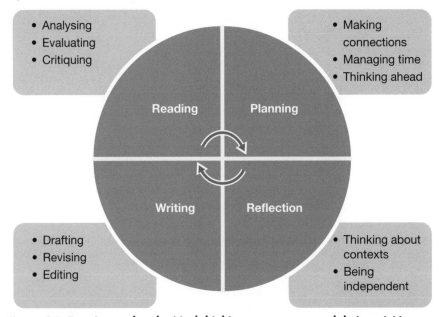

Figure C.1 **Four inter-related critical thinking components and their activities**

In conclusion, critical thinking is about applying your insights to understand topics and generate knowledge. As a critical thinker, you should aim to make a contribution to your community within academia, industry, commerce or whichever environment in which you are operating, but the ways you choose to do this depend entirely upon you.

References

Lunsford, A. A. (2005) *The Everyday Writer*. 3rd edn. Boston: Bedford/St Martin's.

Wallas, G. (1926) *The Art of Thought*. New York: Harcourt Brace.

REFERENCES

Bailin, S. and Siegel, H. (2003) Critical Thinking. In Blake, N., Smeyers, P., Smith, R. and Standish, P. (eds) *The Blackwell Guide to the Philosophy of Education.* Oxford: Blackwell: 181–193.

Bartram, B. and Bailey, C. (2009) Different Students, Same Difference?: A Comparison of UK and International Students' Understandings of Effective Teaching. *Active Learning in Higher Education* 10: 172–184.

Barzilai, S. and Zohar, A. (2006) How Does Information Technology Shape Thinking? *Thinking Skills and Creativity* 1: 130–45.

Cottrell, S. (2005) *Critical Thinking Skills: Developing Effective Analysis and Argument.* Houndmills: Palgrave Macmillan.

Descartes, R. (1637) *Discourse on the Method of Rightly Conducting one's Reason and Seeking Truth in the Sciences.* trans. by Jonathan Bennett (2007). Available from: <http://www.earlymoderntexts.com/pdf/descdisc.pdf> [6 April 2010].

Descartes, R. (1641) *Meditations on First Philosophy in which are demonstrated the Existence of God and the Distinction between the Human Soul and Body.* trans. by Jonathan Bennett (2007). Available from: <http://www.earlymoderntexts.com/pdf/descmed.pdf> [6 April 2010].

Dewey, J. (1997/1910) *How We Think.* Mineola, NY: Dover Publications.

Fiske, S. T., Cuddy, A. J. C., Glick, P. and Xu, J. (2002) A Model of (often mixed) Stereotype Content: Competence and Warmth Respectively follow from Perceived Status and Competition. *Journal of Personality and Social Psychology* 82: 878–902.

Goody, J. (1977) *The Domestication of the Savage Mind.* Cambridge: Cambridge University Press.

Greasley, P. and Cassidy, A. (2010) When it Comes Round to Marking Assignments: How to Impress and How to 'Distress' Lecturers. *Assessment and Evaluation in Higher Education* 35: 173–89.

Haggis, T. (2003) Constructing Images of Ourselves? A Critical Investigation into Approaches to Learning Research in Higher Education. *British Educational Research Journal* 29 (1): 89–104.

Hyland, K. (2002) Authority and Invisibility: Authorial Identity in Academic Writing. *Journal of Pragmatics* 34: 1091–1112.

Kay, J. (2010) *Oblinquity.* London: Profile Books.

Lamb, B. (2009) British Undergraduates Make Three Times as Many Errors in English as Do Ones from Overseas. *Quest*, unpaginated.

Leeds City Council (2010) *Head of information management and technology.* http://jobs.leeds.gov.uk/JobDetails.aspx/5221/Assistant_Commissioning_Officer/?Ssimple=&SSectors=-1&SSalary=-1&STerm=19&Sdepartment_id=-1&SLocations=-1&SSchools=4&SSubjects=&o= [27 March 2010].

References

Lunsford, A. A. (2005) *The Everyday Writer*. 3rd edn. Boston: Bedford/St Martin's.

Nye, J. S., Jr (2004) *Soft Power: The Means to Success in World Politics*. New York: Public Affairs.

Paul, R. and Elder, L. (2002) *Critical Thinking: Tools for Taking Charge of your Personal and Professional Life*. Upper Saddle River, NJ: Financial Times Prentice Hall.

Perkins, D. N. (1985) The Fingertip Effect: How Information Processing Technology Changes Thinking. *Educational Researcher* 14 (7):11–17.

Taylor, L. (2010) Thinking Outside the Box. *The Times Higher Education* 11 March 2010: 43–45.

Wallas, G. (1926) *The Art of Thought*. New York: Harcourt Brace.

Watson, J. D. and Crick, F. H. C. (1953) Molecular Structure of Nucleic Acids. *Nature* 171: 737–738.

Zampetakis, L. A., Bouranta, N. and Moustakis, V. S. (2010) On the Relationship between Individual Creativitiy and Time Management. *Thinking Skills and Creativity* 5: 23–32.

INDEX

abstracts 67, 74–5
  key features 75–6
  keywords 74
adding value 11
analysis 49–50
  strategy for 53, 54, 61
    Descartes' critical thinking method
      55–61
    disciplinary knowledge 54
    judgement in academia 55
  task 66–7
articles *see* journals
assertiveness 96
assignments 50
  demands of academia 9–10
  errors 56–7
  examples of critical thinking 33–6
  informed contribution 28–9
  marking criteria 29, 32, 54
  preparing to write 66
    analysing task 66–7
  purpose of reading 29–30
  revise and edit your writing 60–1
  stance in academic writing 36–9
  student writers 30
  students' knowledge 31–2
  thinking outside the box 30–1
  too descriptive 32, 35–6
attendance at lectures/classes 48, 49,
  54
author–date referencing 19–20
  purposes of date 20–2
  sample article 14–18
    patterns of citations 22–3
authors
  lead 20
  stance 36–9
  websites 23

Bailin, S. 10
bias 59, 79, 80

career 44, 96, 108–9
  ambitions 104

experience 106–8
knowledge 104–7
skills 104–5
disciplinary specificity 69
employer criteria 98
  job description 98–100, 101
  person specification 100–4
  transferable critical thinking skills
    96–8
charities 107
classes 49, 54
closed-minded 89–90
components of critical thinking 44–5,
  51
  analysis 49–50
  career and 96–8
    experience 107–8
    job description 100, 101
    knowledge 104–7
    skills required 104–5
  connections 45–6, 96–8, 104
  context 49, 104
  independence 47, 96, 104, 106
  intellectual development 48–9
  long-term planning 50, 104–8, 108
  reflectivity 46–7, 96, 104, 107
  time management 46, 48, 90, 104, 107
conferences 23
connections 45–6
  career 96–8, 104
context 49
  academia 8–10
  daily life 6–8
contribution
  adding value with critical thinking 11
  informed 28–9
criticising and critical thinking 10
critique your own ideas 59–60
current affairs 49

daily life 6–8
Darwin, Charles 92
databases 23, 67, 69
debate/discussion 46, 54, 59, 60, 89

decision tables 90–2
definitions of critical thinking 4–5
Descartes' critical thinking method
    55–6
  applications of 57–61
  errors
    academic practice 57
    understanding 56
descriptive writing
  excess of 32, 35–6
Dewey, John 4–5, 6
disciplinary specificity 69
discussion/debate 46, 54, 59, 60, 89
dissertations 54
doubt everything 57–8

e-mails 9
  unknown senders 6–8
edit your writing 60–1
elements in critical thinking 5–6
employment *see* career
errors 96
  academic practice 57
  understanding 56
examine other people's ideas 58
examples of critical thinking 33–6

Goody, J. 89
Google 23
Google Scholar 23, 24
Greasley, P. 9, 32, 36

honesty 92
humanities
  databases 23
  journal articles 71
Hyland, K. 37

independence 47
  career 96, 104
intellectual development 48–9
Internet 9
  e-mails from unknown senders 6–8
  source of information 23
interpersonal skills 97

job description 98–100, 101
journals 23–4
  abstracts 67, 74–5
    key features 75–6
    keywords 74

articles
  key features 76–7
  sample *see below*
  structure of 71
conducting research 69–72
Internet pages 23
peer review 70, 74
referencing 18, 72
  author–date 19–22
  numerical 19
sample article, first 14–18, 25
  examining references 18–22
  moving forward 23–4
  patterns of citations 22–3
sample article, second 82–3
  conclusion 82
discussion 81–2
introduction 77–8
limitations 80, 81
literature review 78–9
method 79–80
results 81
judgement
  in academia 55
  time management 48

Kay, J. 92
knowledge
  career 107
  generating disciplinary 54
  moving front of 21
  student 31–2

Lamb, B. 31
lead author 20
lectures 48, 49, 54
library 69, 72
literacy 89
literature review 74, 78–9
  mind map of 22
long-term planning 50
  career 104, 108
Lunsford, A.A. 111

marking criteria 29, 32, 54
mind map
  of literature review 22
moving front of knowledge 21

negotiation 96
networking 96–7, 104

numeric referencing 19

objectives 50
open-minded 89–90

Paul, R. 5
peer review 70, 74
personal development planning 47
personal pronouns 37
planning 112
   components of critical thinking 44–5,
      51
   analysis 49–50
   career and 96–8, 100, 101, 104–5,
      107, 108
   connections 45–6, 96–8, 104
   context 49, 106
   independence 47, 96, 101, 104,
      105, 106
   intellectual development 48–9
   long-term planning 50, 104, 106,
      108
   reflectivity 46–7, 96, 104, 107
   time management 46, 48, 90, 104,
      107
   strategy for analysis 53, 54, 61
   Descartes' critical thinking method
      55–61
   disciplinary knowledge 54
   errors 56–7
   judgement in academia 55

reading 111
   academic context 8–10
   and action 29
   adding value 11
   analyse texts 49–50, 60
   building on scholarship 27, 39
      examples of critical thinking 33–6
      informed contribution 28–9
      purpose of reading 29–30
      stance in academic writing 36–9
      student writers 30
      students' knowledge 31–2
      thinking outside the box 30–1
      too descriptive 32, 35–6
   criticising and critical thinking 10
   daily life 6–8
   efficiently: SQ3R technique 24–5
   lists/recommended texts 47, 69
   purpose of 29–30

sample article 14–18, 25
   examining references 18–22
   moving forward 23–4
   putting information together 22–3
   scanning 68–9
   skimming 68
   SQ3R technique 24–5
   wide 46, 48
record keeping
   journals and their aims 69
   sources 49, 72
referencing 18, 72
   author–date 19–20
      patterns of citations 22–3
      purposes of date 20–2
      sample article 14–18
   list of references 72
   numerical 19
reflectivity 46–7, 113
   career 96, 104
   four steps 88–9, 93
      clarifying your thinking 90–2
      do not be closed-minded 89–90
      look at your questions 89
      sticking to the point 93
research
   conducting 69–72
respect 96
revise your writing 60

scanning 68–9
scepticism 56, 59
   e-mails from unknown senders 6–8
scholarly writing 112
   peer review 70, 74
   reading journal articles 69–71
   sample article 82–3
      conclusion 82
      discussion 81–2
      introduction 77–8
      limitations 80–1
      literature review 78–9
      method 79–80
      results 81
   stance of author 36–9
scholarship, building on 27, 39
   examples of critical thinking 33–6
   informed contribution 28–9
   purpose of reading 29–30
   stance in academic writing 36–9
   student writers 30

students' knowledge 31–2
thinking outside the box 30–1
too descriptive 33, 35–6
sciences
  databases 23
  journal articles 71
  numeric referencing 19
self-awareness 5–6, 92, 96
self-confidence 88
self-criticism 88
skills, work 104–5
skimming 68
social sciences 74
  author–date referencing 19
  databases 23
Socrates 4
sources
  locating and selecting 67–8
  previewing 68–9
  referencing system 18–22, 72
    patterns of citations 22–3
    sample article 14–18
specificity, disciplinary 69
SQ3R technique 24–5
stance in academic writing 36–9
strategy for analysis 53, 54, 61
  Descartes' critical thinking method
    55–6
    applications of 57–61
  disciplinary knowledge 54
  errors
    academic practice 57
    understanding 56
  judgement in academia 55
stress 46
student
  knowledge 31–2
  writers 30
style
  author's stance 37–9

personal pronouns 37
substance and 31–2
surface level, see beyond 61

talk about your ideas 46, 60
Taylor, Laurie 30–1, 32
time 50, 59–60, 67, 70, 112
  limits 89
  management 46, 48, 90, 104, 107
topic sentence 68

value, adding 11
volunteer sector 107–8

Wallas, G. 112
websites
  authors 23
word limits 35
words
  author's stance 37–9
work experience 107–8
writing 66, 72, 112
  analysing task 66–7
  assignments see separate entry
  descriptive 32–3, 34–5
  disciplinary specificity 69
  dissertations 54
  edit 60–1
  referencing sources 18–22, 72
    patterns of citations 22–3
    sample article 14–18
  research 69–72
  revise 60
  scholarly see separate entry
  sources
    locating and selecting 67–8
    previewing 68–9
  stance in academic 36–9
  students 30

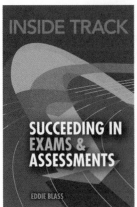